Other Books Edited and Contributed to by Tyler Stallings

Are We Touched? Identities From Outer Space

Cyborg Manifesto, or The Joy of Artifice

Desmothernismo: Rubén Ortiz Torres

Free Enterprise: The Art of Citizen Space Exploration

Gabriela León: Sunday Walk to the Zócalo

Sandow Birk's "In Smog and Thunder: Historical Works from The Great War of the Californias"

The Signs Pile Up: Paintings by Pedro Álvarez

Surf Culture—The Art History of Surfing

Truthiness: Photography as Sculpture

Uncontrollable Bodies: Testimonies of Identity and Culture

Whiteness, A Wayward Construction

Aridtopia

Aridtopia

Essays on Art & Culture from Deserts in the Southwest United States

Tyler Stallings

BLUE WEST BOOKS

RIVERSIDE, CALIFORNIA

Blue West Books

Riverside, California

Copyright © 2014, Tyler Stallings
Printed in the United States of America
First edition, 2014
Front and back cover photos by Tyler Stallings
Cover design by Ben Hatheway

.

ISBN: 978-0-9859495-3-2
LCCN: 2013953055

Blue West Books is a publishing collective dedicated to promoting
emerging and established authors of contemporary fiction, poetry, and
essays in California and the Southwest.

www.BlueWestBooks.com

For Naida.

Introduction 1

Part I: Desert Secessions

Secession in the Desert: How Walking through a Mock Iraqi City
Led to Aridtopia 7

Aridtopia's Loop Writing: A Desert Language 17

Concrete Islands Along California Freeways Jump-Start a New
Society 25

Repurposing the Los Angeles Aqueduct as a Pathway for Sacred
Pilgrimages 31

Part II: Desert Sounds

An Iron Worm Whistles In My Mind 57

Considering the Sound of an Air Conditioner while Perusing
John Cage: Zen Ox-Herding Pictures 67

Area 51: A Sound Installation by Venzha Christ 81

Part III: Desert Architectonics

Pump Up the Realism: Todd Brainard's Paintings 89

Laurie Brown: Recent Terrains 95

Cabins in the Desert: Ruminating on Kim Stringfellow's
Exploration of Jackrabbit Homesteads 101

From Beefcake to Skatecake: Shifting Depictions of Masculinity
and the Backyard Swimming Pool in Southern California 109

Part IV: Desert Planets

Free Enterprise: The Art of Citizen Space Exploration 135

Manifest Destination in *Spaceport America* by Connie Samaras 147

Miguel Palma: An Artistic Exploration of the Sonoran Desert by
a Human Alien 153

A Reconsideration of Fourth of July Fireworks and
Independence Day in Light of Cai Guo-Qiang's *Sky Ladder*   161

Presence Machines: Philip K. Dick's Roman Empire and *The
Imaginary 20th Century*   167

Part V: Desert Mythos

Levitating the Archaic Mind with Michael Heizer's *Levitated
Mass*   175

The Idyll-Beast: A Wild Child Imaginary in Idyllwild, California   185

Lewis deSoto & Erin Neff: *Tahquitz*   193

Resurrection Machines of Ancient Egypt in San Bernardino and
of Ancient Cinema in Hollywood   201

An Inland Empire Afterlife: The Immortality Project, Cryonics,
and a 26-Foot Tall Marilyn Monroe   211

Hell's Union: Motorcycle Club Cuts as American Folk Art   223

Visiting with China's Ancient Terra Cotta Warriors, or Combat-
Ready for Paradise   237

Acknowledgments & Illustrations   243

Index   251

Aridtopia

Introduction

Aridtopia is a state of mind. It is a viewpoint that comes from having thoughts in an arid region. It understands that water is gold. It understands that the desert is a setting for so much that co-exists: survivalists, military bases, legacies of Native American and settler conflicts, water wars, love for open vistas, and full of people who go their to experience the desert's spaciousness in order to reconnect to the vast, cosmic spaciousness beyond this planet.

The spaciousness between vegetation, mountains, and even people allows room for the mind, soul, and sprit to wonder. For centuries, spiritual seekers have gone into the desert. The openness allows for secrecy too. Doomsayers will some times set up their fortresses there, while the military will establish secret operations too.

Since arriving at University of California, Riverside seven years ago, I've had an opportunity to explore the nearby Mojave, Sonoran, and Colorado Deserts. While a magnet for creative types since the 1960s, a plethora of artists and musicians have been moving to Joshua Tree since the 1990s. Some want the opportunity to own a piece of land and spread out, while others view desert solitude and self-sufficiency as beneficial to their artistic practice.

My inspiration for engaging with the desert began when the University of California Institute for Research in the Arts (UCIRA) Desert Studies was launched in 2009 by UC Santa Barbara professor Dick Hebdige in association with UC Riverside's Palm Desert Graduate Center as a UCIRA demonstration project exemplifying the Institute's then new commitment to a Social Ecologies, California-centric embedded arts research program. He had also consulted with Bruce Ferguson at Arizona State University who started an artist-based Desert Initiative program. Their idea, and it is a concept that has remained with me, was to view the world differently through an artistic lens and from the perspective of its numerous deserts, rather than its oceans, forests, or jungles.

However, amidst the nation's economic downturn in 2008, both universities made cuts, which affected both programs. After a year and a half of programming at the UCR Palm Desert campus, Hebdige returned to UC Santa Barbara, while Ferguson went to teach at the American University in Cairo; but the Desert Initiative program at ASU has continued in a different form. Greg Esser now directs it.

He, along with artists Andrea Polli and Kim Stringfellow, are co-editors for *Arid Journal*, which has been the main site where I've developed my thought experiment that I call Aridtopia, a speculative, secessionist community set in the southwest United States. The concept for this environmentally sustainable community in an arid region was inspired by Ernest Callenbach's 1975 novel, *Ectotopia*. That story's setting is the secession of Washington, Oregon, and northern California from the U.S. in order to create what he called a "steady-state" society, a precursor to "sustainability."

Simultaneous to my entries in *Arid Journal*, I was invited by

KCET-TV's *Artbound* program to write a column covering arts and culture in the Inland Empire, a moniker that encompasses cities north of Los Angeles, ranging from Pomona to Riverside to Palm Springs. From the onset, I knew that I wanted to write pieces that would eventually form the majority of the ones found in this collection. Here, I had the latitude to be experimental in my writing style and to do what I love, which is to mash up popular culture, academic discourse, and speculative ideas about society.

The essays under the first section, "Desert Secession," explore Aridtopia directly. The succeeding essays carries an Aridtopian spirit of reframing what one may find in the desert. Since Aridtopia is a secessionist community, it develops its new society, in part, by repurposing what was left behind within its territory. I envision a vibrant sense of innovation, self-sufficiency, and the zeal of starting anew. In general, I do not despair about the state of today's cultural life in these essays. Rather, I wear utopian glasses. For me, there is an opportunity in deserts to find a way to salvage the detritus of society, in order to make a better vision of life, whether for oneself, or across what may one day be a newly established border in the southwest United States for a new society called *Aridtopia*. □

Part I

Desert Secessions

Secession in the Desert: How Walking through a Mock Iraqi City Led to Aridtopia

(2012)

In October of 2009, I had the opportunity to take a tour of the Marine Corps Air Ground Combat Center in Twentynine Palms, California in the Mojave Desert.[1] It was part of a UC-wide project called *Mapping the Desert/Deserting the Map: An Interdisciplinary Response.* I co-organized it with Dick Hebdige from University of California, Santa Barbara, who had hoped to start an artist-based research studies program at UC Riverside's Palm Desert campus[2]. However, the ensuing California budget crisis thwarted the plans. Nonetheless, the Marine mock city has continued to occupy my thoughts in the years that have followed the experience.

Built with shipping containers—the ones that we see on freighters docking in San Pedro or on trains taking those same containers and their goods out on the rail lines that feed the other states--the mock city that I saw was meant to mirror a typical Iraqi one at the time, since we were then at war with that country. Now, I assume that the mock city has since been rearranged, like Lego

---

[1] Watson, Julie, "$170 million mock city rises at Marine base," MSNBC News, January 26, 2011. Accessed on May 30, 2012, http://www.msnbc.msn.com/id/41258569/ns/us_news-life/t/million-mock-city-rises-marine-base/#.T87JdO1uHzl

[2] "Mapping the Desert" was co-organized by Sweeney Art Gallery, University of California, Riverside, and University of California Institute for Research in the Arts (UCIRA), which was co-directed by Dick Hebdige at the time. The related website documents all phases of this project and prior ones for arts-based desert research initiated by Hebdige, http://www.sweeney.ucr.edu/exhibitions/mappingthedesert/.

blocks, to suggest an Afghan one, or perhaps an Egyptian one, maybe even one in Syria. Whatever the city, I assume that it's one in the Arabian or Syrian Deserts.

Our guide said, "Future wars will be fought in cities." His example for other cities was not an Arabian one however. Instead, he said, "We could stack these containers to seem like a city block in Chicago."[3]

I know that he meant to exemplify the heights that the Marine's could reach with their stacking. But, whether he knew it or not, and if he did, perhaps he slipped in sharing his information, it was not to many years after my visit, that the Marines did have an opportunity to occupy Chicago with their mock-ishness.

On April 12, 2012, *The Chicago Tribune* reported that during the preparations for a NATO summit in the city that "as attention on security intensifies, the city announced Monday that a 'routine military training exercise' would be under way in and around Chicago from April 16 to 19 to help personnel preparing for overseas deployment learn to 'operate in urban environments.' A city spokeswoman said the training is done around the country and is not related to the NATO meeting."[4]

Under contract, Lockheed Martin has been building Urban Operations Training Systems all over the U.S. They are often city-

[3] Podcast documentation posted on website for "Mapping the Desert/Deserting the Map: An Interdisciplinary Response," Sweeney Art Gallery, University of California, Riverside. Accessed on May 31, 2012, http://www.sweeney.ucr.edu/exhibitions/mappingthedesert/.

[4] Coen, Jeff and Heinzmann, David, "Chicago preparing for NATO summit," Chicago Tribune, April 16, 2012. Accessed on May 31, 2012,
http://www.chicagotribune.com/news/local/breaking/chi-nato-training-exercises-in-chicago-underway-20120416,0,1795383.story.

size simulation facilities, like the one in Twentynine Palms, to help soldiers maintain their skills that they honed patrolling cities overseas and to prepare for the future.[5]

There are several districts that make up the one in Twentynine Palms, covering 274 acres in the desert. Fake markets, hotels and other businesses are populated with actors who create scenarios, ranging from humanitarian relief efforts to peacekeeping to police work and direct combat. The town can also be populated with up to 15,000 Marines for a training simulation.

The simulations involve not only what the Marines can see, but they are also be trained to find escape tunnels, weapons caches, watch for where the last man in a line could be taken hostage, deal with hidden bombs in what would appear to be abandoned vehicles. There are thousands of linear feet of underground tunnels so that the actors can appear most anywhere throughout the city to simulate a surprise attack. Occasionally, there are shrapnel-free, special-effect explosions to mimic incoming missiles or suicide bombers, perhaps. Either way, you can't trust a carpet seller, right?

Unfortunately, I cannot help but think that Marine's training in both mock cities and real cities, both abroad and domestically, is unsaid preparation for an extended martial law. My gut response is to think that this would be implemented during a financial crisis brought on by diminishing oil supplies. However,

[5] Ackerman, Spencer, "Lockheed Gets Big Bucks to Prep Soldiers for Urban War," Wired magazine, Danger Room column, January 18, 2011. Accessed on June 1, 2012, http://www.wired.com/dangerroom/2011/01/lockheed-gets-big-bucks-to-prep-soldiers-in-urban-war/.

living here on the edge of the Mojave, and thinking about the many arid lands around the world, several of which have been the settings for war, it seems that another resource will be the reason for military occupation: water.

++++

While staying abreast of the mock city construction and mock military exercises in U.S. cities in these past few months, it was during this time that author Ernest Callenbach died on April 16, 2012.

He wrote the novel *Ecotopia*, which he self-published in 1975[6]. It became a cult success, telling the story of a utopian world in which Northern California, Oregon, and Washington had seceded from the United States in order to live in a "steady-state" with the environment, which we call "sustainability" today, or more radically, "permaculture." When he wrote the novel, he was well into his career as the editor of *Film Quarterly*, which he edited for 33 years.

The book was inspired from his desire to write a magazine article about the problem of waste in the consumer society that surrounded him in the early 1970s. Instead, he opted to write a speculative novel about a country that embraced recycling, among other changes in social values. In a sense, the novel became an

[6] Callenbach, Ernest. Ecotopia (Berkeley: Heyday Books, 1975, 30th anniversary edition). http://ernestcallenbach.com/Books.html

extended magazine article, eschewing characterization for observations about this new society, told from the point of view of a reporter from the United States entering into Ecotopia for the first time in twenty years after secession.

Soon after reading *Ecotopia*, I wanted to imitate his action of using writing to bear witness. However, I wanted the setting of my book to encompass a particular location and passion where I live, the arid land of Southern California.

In a true moment of inspiration, the name, "Aridtopia," formed in my mind quickly.

I searched the web for any sign of its use. I found none, which was a surprise to me, as the name had become commonplace in my thoughts already in just a short amount of time. Immediately, I registered the web domain, www.aridtopia.com.

++++

Here is the beginning of defining Aridtopia through fiction, but with the sensibility of a pamphleteer, ranter, and activist:

Aridtopia is a speculative, utopian community in the Mojave Desert. It was founded when parts of southern California and Nevada, along with all of Arizona and New Mexico seceded from the United States to create a "dry-water" ecosystem: a balance between human beings, water, and the desert. It is one of several new nations created after the U.S. federal government abdicated central control in light of economic, environmental, and educational collapses. Today, the U.S. is composed of its original

thirteen states from centuries ago, and has been renamed The
Thirteen United States (TUS). Now, decades later, after The Grand
Secession, Aridtopia is publishing a short history that is for the
benefit of its citizens, its neighbor nations, and The Thirteen United
States. It's also for TUS adherents who live in the new nations, but
hope to reunite the land from Pacific to Atlantic Oceans, as it was at
one time in the near past.

History in Aridtopia is told from personal accounts only.
Individuals are held accountable, not governments, corporations,
families, tribes, or partners.

I will start with a description of where I live. One's
environment and one's spirit are inseparable, although they may
change over time, but in tandem.

I live on a former Marine Corps base in the Mojave Desert,
about 140 miles east of downtown Los Angeles. In the past, First
Nations people would claim certain geographical sites as sacred,
such as mountains, as the source of the birth of their people—
upwelling from the depths of the planet. After The Grand Secession,
Aridtopians decided to repurpose past structures as a way to
repurpose them for a dry-water state but also to rehabilitate the
land, to make it sacred again. Although, not in terms of being a site
of mythical birth, but as a recognized partner in developing a new
life.

I live in what was once a city, but not a city, a mock city for
military combat training in urban settings. Constructed with
stacked shipping containers that are bolted together, they resemble
adobe pueblos of the past, as in the five storied, terraced ones in

the San Juan country in northern New Mexico, like Pueblo Bonito in Chaco Canyon.

When this was an Iraqi mock-village, one side of the central plaza had narrow streets and dense housing to represent the poorer inhabitants, while the other arm that extended from the opposite side of the plaza had wider streets and less dense housing to represent the upper class. These variations allowed for simulations on how to maneuver a tank through varying street widths. We have not such distinctions in the reformed plan. Like kivas in the past, there is no privileged seat. There is no throne.

Aridtopians need to work together a lot. Since life is very communal for now, our homes tend to be small and simple. Instead, the big structures are the Gathering Spots. A couple of hundred years ago in desert towns, such a spot might have been the town saloon--boxes with giant false fronts to suggest grandeur. Inside, you see fancy, carved bars that could be either a place to sip a drink or perhaps a baroque altar. You can see the values of pioneers embodied in the architecture. It was largely men who came out with the shirts on their back to make stakes in mining or ranching. Hard work, hard life, hard drinking. But most of these towns are gone because wood is not native to the deserts, at least not the way it was used for stud and clapboard. Instead, we have centuries-old, adobe cliff dwellings, among other structures, still standing throughout the southwest.

Like the long history of desert architecture, whether ancient, United Statesean, or where I stand now, the main design features in Aridtopia are open plans, in which the interior and exterior flow into one another, but including barriers against the constant and intense sunlight. You see canopies, loggias, and perforated screens everywhere. In fact, most people sleep under them at night rather than within the container of their walls, especially during the summer months.

We Aridtopians look at the teacher-plants around us for inspiration. There's the Saguaro, with its vertical rods, like tendons that hold it upright for years. There's the Cholla with its lattice structure and the Ocotillo with its emergent, tail-like slender stalk, usually over ten feet long, waving in the air under tensile strength.

The steel shipping containers are slowly replaced with less and less rigid walls; flexible ones that have been formed in order to withstand heat, wind, and a lack of precipitation. Cacti and succulents are full of secrets. Or, not really secrets, but simply there waiting for humans to recognize the integrity and strength of their designs.

In general, this approach to architecture is a part of what we call the Sun Agreement. For example, in one of our main squares, there is a giant canopy under which people gather. It is perforated to allow wind to pass through, so as not to tear the fabric, so as to provide shelter from the sun, but allow light to pass through as if through a tree's foliage, and finally to allow birds and insects to dart in and out freely. It is Sympathetic Architecture that works with the Sun, land, and low precipitation.

The world is based on relationships. Nothing happens that is not an outgrowth of relationships. From an Aridtopian viewpoint, the most radical things to do now are to grow your own food, to choose your relationships, to decide how you want to breathe, and to create clean water. It is the end of the Imperial Human.

++++

Next chapter: How someone chose to join Aridtopia? Who was willing to believe in producerism rather than consumerism? Who was willing to get rid of third person narrator and enjoy "I" and "We"? Who was willing to stop watching and start feeling? Who was willing to change their habits? Who felt that they could leave others behind?

++++

This is where my imagination lives now.
"May moisture find you." □

Aridtopia's Loop Writing: A Desert Language
(2013)

Lately, I've been building a world in my mind. It is called Aridtopia.

Aridtopia is a speculative, utopian community in the Mojave Desert. In my fantasies, it was founded when parts of southern California and Nevada, along with all of Arizona and New Mexico seceded from the United States to create a "dry-water" ecosystem: a balance between human beings, water, and the desert. It is one of several new nations created after the U.S. federal government abdicated central control in light of economic, environmental, and educational collapses.

The way of speaking and writing in this new community is explored in this essay. Aridtopians speak and write in a very purposeful manner in order to break from a past language structure. It is akin to new societies creating a new calendar system in order to be clear that the beginning of their society is also Year One within their cosmic scheme.

A mindful Aridtopian writes in a style that is called "loop writing." It involves selecting words and reusing them throughout the text in a manner that will reveal new meaning each time that it is used. In this manner, the power of the word's context is brought to light.

Following, then, is a personal account, using the mindfulness of "loop writing," of watching my significant other set up her photo equipment during a very dark night in Joshua Tree National Park, located in the Mojave Desert. Aridtopians work at night often in order to avoid water loss during the heat of the day. However, most animals, including dangerous ones, like rattlesnakes and scorpions, follow the same timetable. Prowling at night is a shared encounter.

She sets up she sets herself up to set up her tripod that sits it sits on the desert floor where she is set up to sit. The desert floor supports her set up and her sitting with her tripod with her camera with her flash to shoot an ocotillo bush that is an upside down tripod with its tall straight branches protruding from a single point upward its single point set on the desert floor.

This set up does not make sense to her. She triggers her camera on the tripod, directing the flash near the base of the ocotillo. Setting it up to appear as the only plant set up on the desert floor, set up on a planet set up in books as the only planet with life.

This viewpoint of recurrence shares some kinship with ancient Egyptian notions of the sun god, Re. He descends in the west, swallowed by the goddess Nut, fights the snake demon, Apophis, the God of chaos, in the night of the underworld, conquering the snake by cutting off its head. Re is reborn from Nut to rise in the east and begin a new day. Otherwise, without the sun, even in the desert, the Egyptians would have perished because their crops along the Nile River, the world's largest oasis that stretches into the Saharan desert, would not have been possible. Each new day brings new meaning. Each word is full of meanings, encompassing both the underworld and the world of humans. In this respect, Aridtopians use language not only to communicate with one another but also to generate additional unintended meanings during the process of speaking. Aridtopians often report feeling giddy after a conversation because they feel as if the universe has been revealed to them as sentient in of itself when the structure of meaning is laid bare as they talk about mundane acts, such as how energized they feel after drinking their first cup of steeped Mormon Tea twigs.

In the dark night for a fraction of a second before the flash there is also Mormon Tea, creosote, rocks all set up to live on the desert floor before and after the flash that freezes incremental movements of branches that are fractions in her life. Most with leaves that are needles instead to conserve water that could die in a flash that does not freeze but burns with sunlight.

Aridtopians embody this sense of discovery in the clothing they wear. Like the tribes of the Sahara, Arabian and Asian deserts, they prefer wearing wrapped layers of cloth to protect the body from heat and cold and to reduce evaporation through the skin by creating a zone of more humid air around the body. So, to unwrap the yards of clothing is to reveal slowly the human body underneath, as if a cocoon were opened to reveal a butterfly about to emerge. In this respect, Aridtopians are like the Tuareg of Africa, as opposed to the Australian Bindibu who go naked. Each deals with heat and cold in their own way.

Additionally, the cloth is dyed bright hues, such as indigo blue and orange, though they do not correspond to orders in a social hierarchy, just personal preference. The dye has been made so that it rubs off on skin like carbon paper. Then, a wet finger is drawn through one's own inked body to make words and symbols for the most intimate to see only. The words are erased at the end of each month by cleansing with a mesquite-based astringent. It is a literal embodiment of textual strategies.

Next she points her camera away from the desert floor to the night sky that is above not only the desert and her but the ocean and others too. The night sky is pinpointed with stars that cannot be seen from the floor of a lit city whose electric lights are pinpoints forcing your attention on itself as if there is no reason to look up and pinpoint new destinations for humankind. A city lit at night is a twelve-hour flash that is more powerful than what she has set up tonight with her own flash to isolate and pinpoint plants in the darkness that is not the night sky but is the floor of the desert.

The best approach for an Aridtopian writer is to simply start writing. Then, as phrases stand out to them, they begin to incorporate them into new contexts. In this process, intention becomes clear for the writer only at the end, thus, there is a true sense of revelation about the language they are using, and hopefully, by keeping true to a sense of discovery, the reader will also go through the same process.

Aridtopians use loop writing to reveal the hidden meanings in the daily news from the outlaying states that are part of the remaining United States of America. They take articles from a newspaper, applying a "loop," and then reissue to the Aridtopian community via electronic means through the internet. Aridtopians try to avoid using paper due to its scarcity. Solar panels and wind turbines generate electricity. They tend to pull news as it relates to the twenty-two deserts around the world. This in itself is reorientation of socio-political thought.

On June 26, 2012, The New York Times published an article by Karla Zabludovsky, "Learning About Life on Mars, via a Detour to Mexico." The following is a looped rewrite excerpt:

Learning About Life on Mars, via a Detour to Mexico is learning about life in Mexico is learning to learn about life

CUATRO CIÉNEGAS, Mexico — Studying Mars usually involves tilting one's head up toward the heavens where there is no tilt once there as there is no up and down to study until on Mars but one is on Mars in the Chihuahuan Desert in Mexico, where the vast, scorching plain is so inhospitable that one tilts one's head towards the heavens hoping for rain too while looking for the distant planet that is inhospitable like the land below one's feet in the Mexican desert.

Is there, was there, water on Mars or on Earth in the Mexican desert that is Mars on Earth but is there a Martian desert like an Earth desert?

For a moment fluttering life can be seen in her flash in the night that might be considered stardust. She is set up to disbelieve that it is stardust. She is sure that bats are flying around her scooping into their mouths the fluttering life seen for a brief moment being alive. Life that could see her too could kill her life on the desert floor. A rattlesnake can see her life with its tongue that can taste the heat of her body set up on the desert floor where her dead body would be preserved for centuries by the dryness of the desert floor, perhaps to be discovered by Martians, seeking a desert to match one on Mars.

Her life is still standing on the desert floor. She cannot figure out the correct exposure time. Blackness is still in her viewfinder. Standing exposed on the desert floor she is correct to be alive still. Though she cannot figure out how to live in the correct time it takes to be exposed. □

Concrete Islands Along California Freeways Jump-Start a New Society
(2013)

Lately, I've noticed mysterious islands along California freeways. The half circumferences of curving transition ramps from one freeway to the next form their perimeters. Many contain terraces of plants native to this arid region, large rock formations, and gravel pathways. But, I never see their inhabitants.

Perhaps the governor is preparing formerly marginal land for habitation by a sinking middle class? Or maybe they will be sites for more prisons with prisoners kept in check by all seeing motorists? They would first have a low-flying, bird's eye view as they drive above them on freeways supported by high columns, and then keep a watchful eye as they transition downward around the curve of the ramp.

The islands are part of a new freeway beautification strategy, actually, built by the state of California's freeway management department, Caltrans. This sentiment is what I've gathered from statements in which aesthetics are integral to Caltrans' landscape architecture. In a State of California government website a bit of Caltrans philosophy stands out: "We view aesthetic treatment as part of the complete project, not an extra cost added onto the project."

In a 2010 *Press Enterprise* newspaper article, Caltrans District 8 Director Ray Wolfe said, "Drivers get an impression of a community from what they see along the road." However, maintenance requirements have increased as more freeways are built and others are expanded, such as with the interchanges fro the 215-91-60 freeways. Wolfe says that the new strategy is to have more native species that require less water and care taking, along with less palm trees and lush grasses. As he so aptly states, "in a wind-whipped desert area like most of the Inland [Empire] area, it just is not 'what we are.'"

Despite being aware of Caltrans' motivations, the islands remain strange, as they appear ready for habitation because of being constructed and manicured to a point that suggests an urban, pocket park. However, there are never any people taking relief from a difficult culture bound with concrete thoroughfares.

J. G. Ballard's 1974 novel, *Concrete Island*, comes to mind. It is a variation on Daniel Defoe's 1719 *Robinson Crusoe* story in which the protagonist crashes his car and finds himself stranded in one of these islands near an English motorway spur. Past victims, now Island occupants, who wish to remain unnoticed in their newfound paradise on which they have squatted, thwart his escape attempts. They fear that he will expose their stranded, car wrecked life that they have embraced.

But, instead of considering such islands from an accident's accidental vantage point or from a near-future dystopian view, how about one that considers repurposing them actively? It is how someone in my speculative, secessionist desert-based community of Aridtopia would reframe this received landscape that is situated in an arid region. It is certainly the attitude that the artist-urban planning project, *Islands of L.A.*, has taken, though focusing on concrete islands accessible by pedestrians rather than those viewed only through the cinematic-like "screens" of windshields. As stated on the project's website, it "was conceived of as a project to investigate the use and availability of the marginalized yet highly visible public spaces of traffic islands."

For me, and anyone with an Aridtopian viewpoint, these mysterious freeway islands help to jump-start our minds to drive away from known and safe environments and walk towards the unknown with a spirit of exploration.

The Caltrans beautification strategy could be reconsidered as less about pleasing the eyes of a speeding motorist and more about providing a purpose-built, high-concept setting for the motorist to contemplate about what kind of society they would initiate if given a blank slate of an island. How would they start their own country? Would they veer towards the utopian, as in the late-1960s television series *Gilligan's Island*, in which bamboo and palm fronds are the base materials for an infinite amount of contraptions for convenience; or toward the dystopian, letting the primitive, territorial, animal consciousness rise to the surface as in William Golding's 1954 novel *Lord of the Flies*?

I would suggest that people rally and occupy the islands. Instead of the Occupy Movement from 2011, it would be the Concrete Island Crusade of 2013. Instead of squatting in front of seats of power, whether government or corporations, these new inhabitants will simply just start their new way of life. Crops will sprout and huts will be thatched. Perhaps, they will even take control of the freeway transition points, becoming literal gatekeepers, and charge a fee to transition, whether to the next freeway or into a new consciousness?

These concrete islets could form a chain of keys found along the interlocking web of California freeways. Collectively, they could be declared as forming a new, unified country—Aridtopia— like Indonesia's archipelago of 17,500 islands, although bound by desert rather than ocean. Freeway shoulders could be designated as Aridtopian rightaways to the concrete islands. Freeways to Freedom! □

Bishop, meeting spot with Alan Bacock, Big Pine Painte Tribe, discuss repurposing of aqueduct

Big Pine / to Ancient Bristlecone Pine Forest, survivors and adaptors like the Painte, b. th thousands of years in the valley

Owens Valley

intake gates of Owens River into aqueduct

Independence

Sierra

Lone Pine

136

Alabama Hills
Site of Hollywood
Westerns and
ancestral Numa
stories superimposed

Nevada

Aridtopian Salt Structures

Fulgurites in dry lake bed

Keeler
DWP Dust Mitigator HQ

190   to Death Valley

190

Dry Owens Lake Bed

White Mountains

Inyo Mountains

China
Lake
Naval Air
Weapons
Station

rockets
and
missiles
named
after
desert
animals

Los Angeles
Aqueduct

395

Nazca Lines-like
aerial view of
aqueduct

14

Jawbone Canyon

Aqueduct siphon
and fire rings
Site of ritmalized
"dream desert"

o o
o o

Tehachapi
Pass Wind Farm

x x x
x x x

Mojave

Lancaster

14

Pearblossom

18   138

15

Aqueduct
Site that inspires
use of aqueduct
as pilgrimage pathway

A Future Aridtopia Boundary

Repurposing the Los Angeles Aqueduct as a Pathway for Sacred Pilgrimages
(2013)

2013 is the centenary of the Los Angles Department of Water and Power's Los Angeles Aqueduct, an engineer's 223-mile dream. A small fraction, 24 miles, is an open ditch; along with 37 miles of lined channels; 12 miles of steel and concrete pipeline, or siphons; 52 miles of concrete tunnels under the desert; plus the most notable and visible sections, the 98 miles of open-air, concrete conduits. I will be visiting sections of each with the viewpoint of a future Aridtopian, a speculative, utopian, desert-based community that encompasses southern California. In its future, the DWP's aqueduct's water flow will be shuttered as a matter of principal based on sustainability and restitution to the Owens Valley. But, even though it will be dry, it will still exist as The Great Incision in the Mojave Desert, or more simply, the Incision. How could it be repurposed in a way that may reconnect people to the land and the water?

Aridtopia is a state of desert mind. It is a place where the most valuable commodity is fresh water, rather than oil, diamonds or gold. Hot, dry winds; unrelenting sunshine; gritty sand in your crevices; a weathered sign that reads "Tropical Oasis," evoking impossibility. It is a place that is around the world: Mojave, Sahara, Atacama, Arabian, Sonoran, Artic and many other places where precipitation is less than ten percent. Robes; vented hats; snake bite kits; jackets for the cool night since there is little moisture to hold the heat as the sunsets.

++++

The satellite image on my smart phone reveals the linear lines of the concrete aqueduct cutting through the Owens Valley, which I will be driving into soon. An extraterrestrial might consider rightly, while peering through its equivalent of a telescope, that they are canals carrying water across the planet's surface to cities. Their correct estimation would be in contrast to the incorrect interpretation of blurry images of Mars seen through telescopes in the late 1800s, which created optical illusions that suggested crisscrossing canals on the Martian surface, thus, life exists!

Today, as we consider settling the planet Mars or Jupiter's moon, Titan, we ask ourselves—from where will the water come? The next question that we ask: is there life beyond Earth, and does it exist in the harsh conditions of either the remnant of an atmosphere or the frozen seas of methane and ethane? These are the same questions that a nascent city on planet Earth in southern California asked in the early twentieth century.

Los Angeles needed water in order to realize its potential in a near desert environment. From where will it come? The answer was the Owens River. The next question: will this affect life in the Owens Valley? No, as there are only the scattered Paiute and Shoshone people and settler-ranchers using the land.

So, like the potential futures of Mars and Titan, the Owens Valley became a colony of Los Angeles. The city bought the land and the water rights for the Los Angeles Aqueduct that began to flow in 1913. The aqueduct allowed for the growth of Los Angeles from a city of just over 100,000 people on 44 square miles in 1900 to over 500,000 people on 364 square miles by 1920. Rather than terraforming Mars into a human habitable planet, Los Angeles deformed the Owens Valley and reformed itself as a livable city.

++++

I begin my journey on the outskirts of what may one day be Aridtopian boundaries in a former region of the U.S., in order to evaluate the repurposing of the Los Angeles Aqueduct. I drive a silver MiniCooper, near the same size as the Mars Curiosity rover, exploring on Earth an arid landscape and the Incision.

Pearblossom, California, U.S. Route 18

I wear a green baseball cap to protect the beginnings of a bald spot from the sun. My back is perspiring from leaning against a faux-leather car seat, despite wearing a thin, cotton, and plaid buttoned shirt. My vision is blurry intermittingly as my contact lens need to slip and slide across moisture on my eyeball in order to work effectively.

The further I drive away from Los Angeles, towards the Mojave Desert, the more the blue dots of swimming pools disappear from my phone's satellite images. I am leaving my home. The Earth's blue, watery surface registers barely from the Voyager 1's viewpoint of 11 billion miles away. It is about to leave our solar system for interstellar space—the first human crafted device to do so. No more water. No more Earth.

I drive past old, sun bleached, drive-in motels, still advertising free HBO and air-conditioning. There is an erasure of its signs. The lettering fades and peels from the sun, designating what was its past purpose: gas station, motel, roadside bar. The cloudless sky and the relentless sun send text into oblivion. Perhaps this will help the future Aridtopian squat in the questionably abandoned structures and then post a new sign: "Last Border Stop Between Aridtopia and the United States of America."

Heading north on the 18, I turn left onto Longview Rd., prompting by a sign that promoted a section of the L.A. Aqueduct as a fishing spot.

I drive up a paved road into the hills, turning off on a dirt road that leads to the Los Angeles Aqueduct that is not visible from the road. I located it by satellite on my phone. It is so well hidden here. Standing on its concrete banks, I watch the water flow smoothly and constantly. Perfect engineering. No trees on the banks nor boulders in the channel to thwart the pull of water down a steady decline from over 3500 feet in the northern end of the Owens Valley to Los Angeles. The water flows on its own; a visible reminder of an invisible force—gravity. Claims have been made that when it poured fourth in 1913, he announced, "There it is! Take it!" My objective as a future Aridtopian is to reconsider this sentiment. One day, I may stand upon a purposefully dry aqueduct and announce, "There, it was never meant to be!"

The cement aqueduct is a miniature valley. Its hard, sloping cement walls are like the steep, sheer grades of the Sierra Nevada and the Inyo White Mountains in the Owens Valley, with the once fertile valley between them. It would be hard to pull myself out if I fell in because there is so little that can be grabbed. I suppose that I would float downstream, like a new day Huckleberry Finn, meeting characters of the desert along the way, until I slid into one of the several reservoirs along the aqueduct's route. And just as Mark Twain's character satirized old, deep-rooted attitudes by Southerners pining for the days before the Civil War, I will become known as No-Job Mesquite, and will offer scathing observations on entrenched views toward water-use.

++++

If the aqueduct were dry, then it could provide a protective trade route between Aridtopia and this region against the desert heat since it is below ground, and nighttime cool temperatures, since the cement will radiate heat absorbed from the sun. Vendors can set up shop too alongside the upper banks. A narrow track can be laid down the center whereby gravity can pull carts down. Another track can be for carts pulled upslope with ropes.

Creosote bush, Mormon Tea shrub, and Mojave yucca surround the cement aqueduct with its deep, flowing water. They are spaced apart, creating less competition for water and mineral resources. The Paiute, who were the first inhabitants of the valley, once lived spaced apart in smaller family units. The Cahuilla in southern California did too. They divided when the group reached around 200 or so. The idea of living as a larger tribe was forced by settler governments that wanted to keep them in one area instead of being able to roam the countryside. I hope that the Paiute, or the Numa, as they call their people, and future Aridtopians will be able to live by their own fates, and not have to surrender to dense living conditions.

Centuries ago, water flowed into imperial, ancient Rome from the countryside via beautifully engineered, arched aqueducts. Los Angeles is imperious too, treating the Owens Valley as a resource-colony. The concrete aqueduct is a prison for the water. The snowpack—the blood of the mountains—is being drained slowly.

I am sweating profusely in the near one hundred degree July heat in the Mojave Desert. A lizard scrambles along the concrete embankment. I will not allow my water to drain from me into the aqueduct.

Jawbone Canyon, northeast of Mojave, California, U.S. Route 14

I drive north from Pearblossom, past the town of Mojave and the Tehachapi Pass Wind Farm—hundreds of single and double blade turbines spinning in the wind--and pull off at Jawbone Canyon, named for hills that resemble mandibles. In the 1800s, several gold mines dotted the landscape. Now, it's the site for one of the largest sections of the LA Aqueduct's metal siphons.

A stark, white line crosses the desert surface. It is one segment of a miles long, nearly seven-foot circumference, metal pipe, or siphon, transporting water from the Owens Valley River to Los Angeles. The siphon's extreme straightness suggests a contemporary rendition of the ancient Nazca Lines in Peru, which often took the shapes of regional animals; some seemingly visible from an aerial viewpoint only. Zigzags of this same pipe are atop hills in the distance; perhaps suggesting a slithering rattlesnake over the landscape, at least as seen from the sky, or the satellite image on my phone. The reflection of the sun off the chalk-like paint covering the pipe is blinding. I walk across the powdered desert sand to touch its side. No sensation of rushing water—of the Sierra Nevada's blood—beneath the metal, as I had expected.

Several fire rings are near the siphon. They are made from nearby, stray stones, and placed in a circle. They are left by what I call "desert-reckers" (those who use the desert for recreation, such as off-roading vehicles, commiserate with the federal policy for parks that states "Land of many uses." An Aridtopian might define it as "wreck-reation"). I imagine them as demarcating one of many resting places for future, Aridtopian pilgrimages along the aqueduct's route.

The Mojave Desert is a land of many uses: people retreat into it for the landscape's solitude, quietness, and stillness, seeking spiritual replenishment. The U.S. military has installed several bases such as Edwards Air Force Base, just south of Jawbone Canyon, or China Lake, north of here in the Indian Wells Valley, just before entering the Owens Valley. There is plenty of land for secrecy and distance from a civilian population for their protection. Experimental rockets and planes do blow up and they crash hard.

How could these siphons be repurposed? The first idea that comes to mind is that they could provide a pathway from Aridtopia into Owens Valley that would provide even more protection from the elements than the open-air cement aqueduct sections that I saw earlier in Pearblossom.

With the siphons, ventilation slits could be cut into their metal sides so that air circulates continuously. This will allow pilgrims and travellers to traverse the desert in coolness. Doorways would be cut into the sides so that people can enter and exit at will, perhaps to sit around one of the fire rings. Flat platforms could be erected atop the curved surface so that people could climb out and up on to them for camping at night from snakes, coyotes, and scorpions.

However, this seems like only practical suggestions. I feel that there's an opportunity to use the aqueduct for enacting a sacred journey, seeking spiritual truth. Maybe it could be a journey that the youth will take as they transition into "deserthood?" It would be like walking in a dream as they walk in the pitch darkness of the siphon with their eyes wide open; severing their tie with the outside world. It would be a waking "dreamdesert" ritual.

Keeler, California, located on the east side of Owens Lake, U.S. Route 395

I leave my Aridtopian fantasies behind at Jawbone, finally merging onto the 395, heading further north into the Owens Valley. I drive past the Naval Air Weapons Station China Lake on my right, or east side, in Indian Wells Valley. It's the Navy's largest base and the source for a variety of rockets and missiles with desert animal inspired names, such as Sidewinder and Shrike. The first is a venomous pit-viper and the second is a bird known for its feeding habit of impaling lizards and insects on the thorns of plants or barbed-wire fences, given them the nickname, "butcher bird." Whether Nazca Lines, lengthy metal pipes carrying water, or missiles, desert animals are a source of representing otherworldly power.

Finally, I reach the southern tip of the desiccated Owens Lake. I turn right off the 395 onto the 190, which curves around the lake's east side, reaching an intersection, where if I continue on 190, I'd enter into Death Valley, but if I turn left on 136, then I'll continue skirting the perimeter of the lake, until I reconnect with the 395 at its northern end.

My MiniCooperMarsRover curves around the depleted, dusty, briny Owens Lake. Large expanses of salt flats are towards its center. When there is some rain, the water mixes with the salt and other minerals, making a small brine pond sometimes. Brine-fly larvae from its edges once sustained the Paiute. But, there is no more water. No more reflections of the sky on a shimmering, undulating, liquid surface.

The lake's main contribution for decades has been alkali dust storms, since the aqueduct began tapping the Owens River above it. As much as four million tons of dust blows off the lakebed, spreading throughout the United States as one the country's largest polluters.

I pass the DWP's Dust Mitigation headquarters. They dump gravel, encourage some vegetation growth, and spray water, to tap down the dust. The process has been successful to a degree, but has cost over a billion dollars, and has been executed only because of a court order.

I driver further north, and then stop at Keeler, midway on the east side, off the 136. Stepping out of my MiniCooperMarsRover, I walk among dilapidated, petrified, sucked dry homes. The upkeep of some places suggests habitation, but it is still a ghost town, but one of hopes and dreams turned into dust. It was built when the Cerro Gordo silver mine was active from 1866 to 1957; 9000 feet up into the hills from here. The ore was once brought down for smelting in Keeler, and then mule trains would take tons of silver to Los Angeles.

I come upon a post and lintel entrance to nothing. The lintel is a surfboard that is a sign, which reads, "Keeler Beach. Swim, Surf, Fish. Camps For Rent." There is no more shoreline since there is no more water.

Keeler and Olancha, on the west side, off the 395, could become sites where pilgrims rest. Perhaps there are areas of the lake that could be sectioned off with walls, so that water can be pumped in, mix with the salt, and create a density of eight times more salt than the ocean, like that of the Judean Desert's Dead Sea. Then, pilgrims could float buoyant on it, their bodies touching nothing hard, loosing sense of their own body, confronting their primal self as the interior and exterior boundaries with the body dissolve into the briny water.

Or, perhaps Aridtopians can specialize in huge salt sculptures. The old smelting kilns for the silver ore could be use to prepare a salt solution: bring a vat of water to a rolling boil, keep adding salt until no more salt will dissolve, add food coloring. Then, bring the vat out onto the salt plains of the lake, build a skeletal wood structure over it, dip rope into the vat, then pull it out so that one end of it dangles in the vat and tie the other end is tied to a spot on the skeletal structure, and then leave it undisturbed. When the salt water begins to cool, the salt molecules will crystallize back into a solid, creating long salt, multicolored, stalagmites along the rope, eventually becoming a crystalline superstructure in the desert. Temporary sanctuaries can be built in this manner. Maybe even a whole city for pilgrims on the dry Owens Lake.

Clues to the past can be excavated in the form of fulgurites, while these Aridtopian structures are being built for the eventual future.

I read once that in the early 1990s, Dr. Scott Stine, a paleoclimatologist at California State University at Hayward, examined centuries-old tree stumps at Mono Lake, now exposed after water levels dropped as the Los Angeles Aqueduct drained water from the Owens Valley. He was able to demonstrate with this evidence that long drought periods are the norm in the California region. The relative wet period, which is coming to an end, and in which we now live, is the anomaly.

He gathered additional evidence from fulgurites at Owens Lake, which are glassy structures in which sand has been fused from lightning strikes, and became accessible after the disappearance of the lake because of the aqueduct. He found fulgurites from both past decades and centuries past, whose trapped electrons allowed for dating further back than expected. This suggested that the lake had been dry many times earlier during which a lightning strike would have had the opportunity to hit a dry lakebed, thus, creating the fulgurites. In other words, there were many, long-lasting droughts in the past. Pilgrims could treat the fulgurites as talismans.

Bishop, California, U.S. Route 395

After Keeler, I skirt the remaining east perimeter of Owens Lake, intersecting with the 395 again. Then, I drive straight through the small towns of Lone Pine, Independence, and Big Pine, arriving in Bishop. It is located above the aqueduct's intake gates, where water begins to flow from the Owens River into it, bypassing the Owens Lake. The river can be found in its unchanneled state in this area.

I pull into Bishop, the biggest town along the 395. Along the main street, are coffee shops and outfitters for hiking, skiing, and camping around Mammoth Lakes, which is located just a little further northwest in the Sierra Nevada. I'm now a couple of a hundred miles north of my starting point in Pearblossom.

I stop at the Black Sheep Espresso Bar to meet with Alan Bacock. He is the Water Program Coordinator for the Big Pine Paiute Tribe of the Owens Valley; tasked with overseeing water quality and quantity for the reservation. I've come to discuss the repurposing of the aqueduct as route of pilgrimage, in light of considering myself as a future emissary from Aridtopia. I am curious as to the options that Alan and the other Paiute, or Numa, may propose for the aqueduct, especially since they were the valley's first inhabitants. They have lived and survived in the arid environment for thousands of years before settlers arrived in 1859.

An initial idea is that the dry aqueduct becomes a causeway between Aridtopia and the Paiute, assuming a possible collegiality based on a mutual respect for the land, and would hence collaborate in the development of a new matrix for the landscape.

I will even suggest that future Aridtopians will assume that in the wake of their future Grand Refusal of the Aqueduct that the Numa may be able to take back the 90% ownership in the land by the settler-DWP, and then evict peacefully the remaining settler-ranchers in the Owens Valley.

The Numa may choose to return to an ancestral method of creating canals that branched off the river creeks flowing from the Sierra to water fields. Places in the Owens Valley may even revert back to being historic gathering spots for the Numa; returning to a lifestyle of constant movement based on seasons by living in temporary dwellings.

++++

Alan and I order coffee and then step out to the Black Sheep Espresso Bar's back porch area to sit under an umbrella, shielding us from the sun. Alan is a young man and has a family. His hair is black and his skin is tanned. He checks his smart phone often, looking for messages from his wife, daughter, or other Paiute.

We had hoped that it would be a quite location so that we could hear each other's comments, but a group sits at another table a few feet away. They seem to be friends who haven't seen each other for a while. A couple is from Australia and another woman has just returned from travels in South Africa. Either the world is becoming one big desert or inhabitants of one desert region are attracted to arid regions elsewhere. Maybe there's an innate feeling that as fresh water becomes a valuable resource it will then become a source of conflict too. This means that adapting to aridity will be important. So, perhaps Alan and I, along with our neighboring group, sipping on iced coffees and spinach smoothies, sense the need to learn desert survivalist skills.

Alan provides some history of his people in the valley. My words are in alternating sans-italics, which are digested reactions that came later to my mind while driving back south on the 395.

Alan: Long ago, our ancestors realized that water did not come from the sky but flowed from the mountains. They learned long ago to build canals and ditches to irrigate seed lands from the Sierra runoff. There were no fences or property lines so when settlers came they thought that the land was not being utilized but it was—by us.

Invisibility does not mean lack of presence.

Alan: In the past, most of the skirmishes with the settlers had to do with food. The livestock were eating plants that we had cultivated and gathered, such as Blue dicks. We would dig them up and gather the corm. Our most important item were the pinyons from the Inyo and White Mountains. There are still some that are being harvested by the Numa. And then the animals were small game that could not get around anymore, due to fences, or livestock taking their food away, so starvation began to happen for us. Then, as we were starving we might kill a cow, for example, and then the rancher would retaliate. Then the military would come in from Fort Independence to protect the settlers. I'm jumping around here on history but you get the point. It's been a slow dwindling of resources. But, we've survived.

To build a fence is to steal from the land. A fence makes one loose one's soul to the impossibility of containment.

Alan: But the Paiute are adaptive. So they adjusted to the new paradigm. This was in the 1860s. Then later the aqueduct brought a second paradigm because there were no jobs with the ranchers since they weren't getting water either. We've always existed, just like the Ancient Bristlecone Pine. I think that you should visit them because they are the oldest living trees, going back 5000 years or more. They have survived in the most extreme of circumstances. Very little water, poor soil, and constant wind. They are like the Paiute; we still live here and still exist, even though many people have tried to destroy us.

Our people have always used the resources, but not to their limit because we live within it. All things are connected. Our use of water affects vegetation, animals and other people. We definitely see things as sacred. So with that point of view, we will always have a different outlook not only towards water, but life.

2013 marks not only the hundred-year anniversary of the LA Aqueduct but it also marks 150 years when our people were forced marched from Fort Independence to Fort Tejon. We just recently had a gathering praying for peace and for the land. In fact, I have a friend who is not native, and who is walking from Fort Tejon to show the forced march in reverse, that is, to show better outcomes can happen, even today.

Aridtopians will walk the dry aqueduct, upstream, against gravity, to reverse the bad intentions connected to decades of water flowing downstream to Los Angeles.

++++

Alan and I depart after talking about ninety minutes. He checks his phone for more messages. He suggests that I drive to the nearby Owens Valley Paiute-Shoshone Cultural Center & Museum.

I realize that people come with answers and not questions many times, when I consider Alan's comments. And, as Alan said during our conversation, "to come with answers often leads to genocide." He even spoke about his missionary work in Japan and how he did not like using the word, "missionary," as it suggests that one is coming with a mission, that is, with solutions ahead of time. I consider a better Aridtopian title might be "questionary," that is, someone who comes into unfamiliar territory with questions in order to learn, rather impose rule.

Toward the end of our conversation, Alan admitted that he's not sure how to respond at the moment to the possibility of the aqueduct being "shut off" in terms of what it would mean for his people, the Numa.

We did not discuss it, but having done a little research on the Numa, I am wondering if some form of forgiveness towards the creation of the L.A. Aqueduct can occur, so as to shed pain and suffering for everyone's present day identities. Perhaps the Numa could line the banks of the aqueduct and enact their mourning ceremony known as the cry dance. Normally, it concluded the mourning of relatives who died during the year before.

But in this case, the cry dance would be ending 150 years of mourning their forced marches, of being put on reservations, and of the water being sent away to a city that does not get rain either. Their tears would fall into the dry, cement aqueduct, filling it with hope and courage. The water would spread out in the valley, creating marshes once again, bringing back the green space; that fertility that so surprised the settlers 150 years ago as they crossed over from the sunburnt, brown Basin or from a fried Sacramento. It would go down in Numa lore as The Great Dry Cry.

Lone Pine, California, U.S. Route 395

My last break before I drive nonstop back over the imaginary U.S./Aridtopia border is in Lone Pine, one of the larger towns, though quite still small, along the 395 in Owens Valley, with Bishop being the other large town at the other end.

Lone Pine is a one stoplight, Main Street town. Just as Bishop is the entryway to Mammoth Lakes, Lone Pine is the entryway to hiking Mount Whitney.

The Lone Pine Indian Reservation is home to Owens Valley Paiute and Shoshone members, and is along the south side of town on both sides of the 395. The Lone Pine Museum of Film History is also located at the south end of Main Street. It's an old movie house with a towering marquee on its façade and has the snow capped Sierra Nevada as its cinematic backdrop.

The museum features exhibitions on the numerous western films shot in the Alabama Hills since the early twentieth-century. I walk through displays on Fatty Arbuckle, John Wayne, Hopalong Cassidy, and The Lone Ranger, between other singing cowboy and perfect-teeth, barely soiled cowboy heroes. The Alabama Hills also served as northern India, the Gobi Desert,

Arabia, and Africa. I drive down Lone Pine's Main Street, drive west up Whitney Portal Road, then turn right onto a dirt and gravel path, staked with the sign, "Movie Road," and follow my map to film locations in the hills.

I drive up a slight incline, then consult my map, and find the site of the tent city that housed the cast and crew for *Gunga Din*. The movie was an adventure tale set in 19th century India. According to my guide map, it was about three raucous British soldiers, and their water bearer, Gunga Din, who must stop an uprising by an Indian cult.

These hills are also the site for ancestral stories by the Numa. They include one about a giant who once pounced through them, screaming to scare people out of their hiding places, then picked them up and killed them. On his way back up the valley, a water baby in the Owens Lake outsmarted him, dragged him into the lake, and drowned him. The stories are about water, whether Gunga Din or a water baby.

I consider the importance of a sense of place as I stand here amidst the rounded boulders, superimposing the stories that are centuries apart. I am developing a story about the aqueduct, the Paiute, and Aridtopia. This place will be here still when the chronology of these stories pass, leaving them to exist all at once in this place.

Alan and I talked about this notion a bit in our conversation in Bishop. On one level, the Paiute stories serve a practical purpose: told as warnings to young kids to stay away from places where they might drown by scaring them with a water baby creature; or as a mimetic device for remembering the location of sources of water and food. But, more importantly, the focus on place connects a person with the land itself, rather than emphasizing movement from place to place as an area is exploited for its resources, until dead as a source of food, water, and memory.

Focusing on place, rather than time, is one of the biggest mental obstacles for future Aridtopians, since we will have once lived in the United States, where "time is of the essence" and "time is money." It has been said that "time heals all wounds." Aridtopians may rephrase this sentiment to read as "place heals all wounds."

In my mind, for future Aridtopians, and for the Numa, perhaps, the LA Aqueduct has been repurposed conceptually. It has been transformed from an immense mechanism for transporting water into one for transporting one's spirit. The Incision would become a sacred pathway for rediscovering one's place within the universe by reconnecting with the land and the water; a desertdreamtrek where one's consciousness dissolves in the liquid cosmos from which all life has emerged. □

Part II

Desert Sounds

An Iron Worm Whistles In My Mind
(2011)

The whistle of a metal worm seeps into my ears. As I lay on my bed at night, staring at the ceiling, here in the city of Riverside, the worm rolls along metal tracks. It wails mournfully in the far distance.

The worm is a train. It sounds like a singular, metallic creature, but in fact the clickclackclickclack on the tracks is composed of many trains in close succession as they enter and exit the city; giving the impression of an endless, thousand-mile, segmented body. Their whistles are ceaseless, as they blow at every grade intersection warning automobile drivers and pedestrians.

The train has been referred to as an Iron Horse. This is due mainly to steam power being defined in terms of the horsepower that once dominated transportation, and presumably because of the clickety-clack of the wheels over the rail joints. But for me, the train is as dominant in this city as it was in the nineteenth century. It is insidious with its whistle winding its way into my mind. For this reason, I see it as a worm, an underground creature, not a mammal like a horse, winding its way down my ear canal.

I've never lived in a town where the trains, or their whistles more specifically, are constant characters. I think that it is why there has never been the image of a train in my dreams. However, the whistles of the two transcontinental rail lines—the Burlington Northern and Santa Fe Railroad and the Union Pacific

Railroad—that trisect Riverside (even vivisect when it comes to my brain being kept awake by click clack, wooooo woooo), are such dominant sounds that they insinuate themselves into both my waking and dreaming lives now.

This "train whistle constant," as I've come to call the phenomenon, does not bother me actually. In essence, just as the sound of the whistle shapes this city, it hones me too. I never "loose my train of thought," literally, by living in Riverside. In fact, I feel as though it provides an aural beacon that keeps my mind steady.

Train Whistle Constant

Riverside once hailed the train. It brought settlers and the cargo here to the edge of Los Angeles. It took the city's products, namely its citrus, to elsewhere. And so the city prospered. The town has grown to a point where the tracks, once on the outskirts, are now in the middle of town. This shift in its urban landscape is the reason that the whistles now emanate from the center of town and can, thus, be heard from anywhere in the city.

Each year, flatbed train cars carry over 700,000 double-stacked cargo containers from the coastal ports of San Pedro, through inland Riverside, into the Mojave Desert, skirting Las Vegas, spreading throughout the Midwest via feeder lines, and arriving at the east coast eventually. As to their contents, my feverish imagination veers between the transportation of spent nuclear rods to quarantined extraterrestrials.

The closest tracks are a mile away, yet the whistles sound so close. My hypothesis is that the hills around my house contain and bounce the sound around, as if we were in an amphitheater. All the residents are forced into being unwilling audience members. We listen to the ongoing drama of the Industrial Revolution as the nineteenth century stretches into the twenty-first.

A Whistle's First Expression

Originating in England in 1832, the train whistle was not invented in order to seep into my dreams or to express emotions for the machine. Rather, it was invented as a warning device and as a way to communicate to other workers up and down the rail. Train whistles exist to this day as a warning device for one reason alone—they are inexpensive when compared to other options, such as raising the rails above the intersecting roads used by cars.

In the past, with steam whistles, an engineer would have some opportunity to be expressive. A pull cord would allow them to vary the rate at which steam was released therefore they had some control. Later, pushbuttons were introduced, which took away the possibility for nuance. Both the old steam whistle and the current compressed air whistle both waver in pitch too, suggesting a cry or wail. Different whistle sounds were created for different train lines in the U.S. in order to distinguish them, ranging from high pitched to deeper tones. The Union Pacific line that runs through this city was once known for their chimes that sounded like a steamboat.

In the past, the different combination of long and short whistles created a code for messages that could be heard down the line. Radio communication is used today mainly. Nonetheless, some of the signals are used still. In the U.S., for example, a combination of two long whistles, followed by a short whistle, then followed by another long whistle, indicates that the train is approaching a public grade crossing. This warning is the source for most whistles heard in cities and for complaints by residents to city councils.

I think about babies in Riverside, born into the sound of the whistle. It is like a coal mine or sawmill company town in the past where the steam whistle predominated and determined the start of the day, breaks, lunch time, and day's end. It was a constant reminder of being part of the machine that determined the town's livelihood, with no opportunity provided for a response, not even a collective whistle back from puckered lips.

The whistles are like church bells, although they ring on the hour from their steeples instead of being constant. However, the capitals of commerce come to mind with the train whistles, rather than they being reminders of spiritual sanctuaries. They evoke the ghosts of English coal mines in the seventeenth century that sought a less expensive method for pumping out water that flooded into them, thus, came the invention of the steam pump. It led to boiler technology and eventually to steam powered trains and their accompanying steam whistles to warn pedestrians to move off the tracks of capitalism making its way through England and Europe. Although, it would be America that would later lay more tracks than its Western cousins laid all together.

The Sound of Melancholia

For some, hearing the "train whistle constant" may produce nostalgia for a love affair with machines. But by the mid-1950s, the dominance of steam trains among commercial and passenger lines waned. Perhaps, this outcome contributes to today's associations of melancholy and loneliness with the train?

Why does the whistle sound melancholy? I think that it has to do with signifying "the end" of something, at least as depicted in movies: two lovers separating at the train station or hobos (now today's homeless) running alongside the tracks and trying to jump into an empty cargo car. But that was when there were boxcars that men at stations had to load and unload which provided an opportunity for stowaways to jump aboard. Now, the cargo trains use standardized, sealed containers mostly, which can be unloaded from ships at port by cranes, loaded onto train cars, and then unloaded onto individual flatbed eighteen-wheelers; and they never have to be opened. No one could get inside of them and if they did then they would suffocate more than likely.

The whistles sound lonely to an everyday listener like me. Their sounds are like a hard luck robots whistling to keep themselves company as they head into the desert. They move from station to station with no time to stop for love. It is as though they mourn their expulsion from an Eden in which human and machines were once together, but have since been separated from one another. Seemingly, the train wants communion with humans again, and its whistle is the melodic lure for reconnection.

Occupied by this cyborgian fantasy, I can rest easy now, as my mind and soul can leave behind identification with the amniotic fluid of a biological birth, a place where the sound of a mother's heartbeat once dominated, and embrace the ambient and ceaseless soundscape of the train whistle.

Soundscape

Since today's trains do not consist of boxcars that I could jump in and ramble across the U.S., I can't imagine being like Delta blues legend David "Honeyboy" Edwards. He road the rails for thirty years, traveling from Mississippi to Chicago, "roamin' and ramblin'," as he sung, playing his harmonica.

Like a song, the train whistle is not a single note, but a chord, made of two or three notes. Musicians and songwriters have included or referenced the sound of the train whistle in their songs for decades, like the numerous ones by Johnny Cash or Boxcar Willie. Or the well-known songs like "I've Been Working on the Railroad," "The Wabash Cannonball," and "The Ballad of Casey Jones." Some songs act as reminders of a life outside of prison walls, as avenues to adventure, as symbols of the achievements of industry, and also of the disasters of collisions and exploding boilers.

However, I'm more interested in sound work that takes not the train whistle's musical quality as a starting point, but rather takes its invasive quality in the aural landscape as found sound. I think of mid-twentieth century French composer, Pierre Henri Marie Schaeffer, an early pioneer with the avant-garde music known as *musique concrete* that utilizes real-world sounds. *Étude aux chemins de fer*, or Railroad Study (1948), features recordings of noises made by trains running on railroad tracks, as a way to bring awareness of the "music" of the city. Several decades later pioneering composer for minimal music, Steve Reich created *Different Trains* (1988) for string quartet and tape, which combined train sounds on tape and sampled train whistles. In the work he uses their sounds to compare and contrast train sounds he heard while a child from 1939-41 in the U.S. with those that might have been heard by prisoners on the way to Nazi death camps during the same period in Europe.

These works bring attention to the symbolic quality of train sounds in particular historical periods and heighten the awareness of sound by asking implicitly, what is "music?" In a broader, philosophical context, they question how definitions and categories are determined.

Whistle Zen

The constancy of the sound is similar to the experience of living in an ocean beachfront town. The crashing of the waves is ever present and dominant. It is an oceanic experience of infinity and eternity that makes me not care about the beginning of anything, whether Adam and Eve or The Big Bang, because the sound evokes a sense of "nowness" as the new norm.

I attribute this nowness to a kind of oneness with the machine via its whistle. In spite of viewing myself as part of a machine in this manner, I feel less like a cog in the proverbial wheels of commerce. This is a reversal from my earlier feelings about being moored to the nineteenth century's soot, child labor, and unwieldy transformation of society by the Industrial Revolution; symbolized by the steam-powered locomotive. I've found a way to approach a sound that people have complained about since the arrival of the train with the intention of using it for another, more personal reason. I've appropriated the incessant train whistle as my personal soundtrack in order to keep me on track of living with awareness and intention.

The whistle, ephemeral as it is, remains in the mind, more permanent that the planned obsolescence of the appliances shipped into the city by the trains. Listening to the whistle provides a transformative experience. The train whistle constant does help as a kind of citywide metronome to keep one's *mindfulness* from derailing.

I have a firmer idea of what I'm hearing now. I don't need earplugs anymore. It's all music now. There is no such thing as silence, not even in one's own mind. □

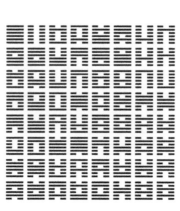

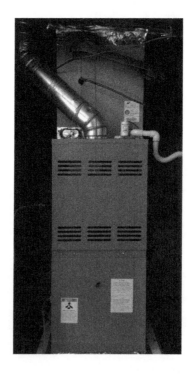

Considering the Sound of an Air Conditioner while Perusing *John Cage: Zen Ox-Herding Pictures*

(2012)

John Cage was a composer, philosopher, writer and visual artist whose interest in East Asian and Indian philosophy led him to renounce artistic intention and instead embrace process and chance in music, performance and visual art. In honor of the centenary of John Cage's birth, the Pomona College Museum of Art presents the traveling exhibition *John Cage: Zen Ox-Herding Pictures* through December 16, 2012. The exhibition brings together 55 watercolors made on brown paper towels, created by Cage in 1988 at the Mountain Lake Workshop in Blacksburg, Virginia. Initially, they were simply used for wiping watercolor brushes, that is, they were not intended as final works. But, as this exhibition demonstrates, most anything can be considered art—in the most positive sense--based on intention and context. The process behind their making and their inspiration also exemplifies the influence on his life of work of Zen Buddhism, which emphasizes that enlightenment can be achieved through a personal path, eschewing doctrine, but emphasizing dialogue with a teacher.

Born in Los Angeles in 1912, Cage attended Pomona College from 1928 to 1930. After a trip to Europe, Cage returned to the U.S. in 1931, eventually turning to music and art, studying with composers Richard Buhlig, Henry Cowell, Adolph Weiss and Arnold

Schoenberg. In 1952, at Black Mountain College, he presented a theatrical event considered by many to have been the first Happening, a performance or event that purposefully eliminates the boundary between the artwork and its viewer in which the two are inseparable in the works execution. *4'33"* was written by Cage and performed by David Tudor sitting without playing in front of a piano for four minutes and thirty-three seconds. It is considered one of the most famous and important pieces in 20th-century avant-garde music and art. In essence, Cage's intention was the creation of an event in which the sounds of the environment gained importance for the listener, as act of active listening and mindfulness.

++++

As I walk through the exhibition, one of two people in the galleries on a Saturday afternoon, reading translations of the Ox-Herding poems, John Cage's poetic aphorisms, and think of reconsidering my own paper towels before I discard them, I find myself considering the difference between the interior and exterior sounds of the building that house the galleries—perhaps charged with knowing of Cage's legacy of, as he says, "to let the sounds be themselves." This attentiveness to auditory margins is inspired also by Cage's use of chance operations in the creation of his compositions.

This overall lingering sensibility of being awake to subtle sounds remains with me throughout the day.

Back home, alone in the house, I find myself attuned to the sounds of the forced air through the ductwork. Its constant, unwavering resonance is calming. All other noises are silenced because of its delicate howl, as if standing in a forest atop a mountain. The windows are shut in order to retain the cool air, which also keeps exterior rattles at a distant too.

I have not lived in a house with air conditioning for decades because of living closer to the coastline in the past. The breezes from the ocean cannot leap the mountain range around Riverside, where I've lived for the past few years now. In the August and September months, the temperatures are in the low 100s. The latter month being the one in which Cage was born (September 5, 1912), hence the celebrations now, and the former month is when he died (August 12, 1992). Somehow, the coincidence of his birth and death months with the hottest months in Riverside, which necessitates running the air conditioner more than I like, seems appropriate to creating conditions for listening to the artifice of the forced air, but trying to accept rather than reject what it has to offer in its unintended mechanical composition.

A downside in using the air conditioner is that it creates a dry environment throughout the house. But, then again, this lack of moisture reflects the outside desert environment—a geographic region that receives less than ten inches of annual precipitation defines a desert. This seems appropriate since deserts are often the sites of spiritual journeys; thus, the air conditioner serves both the purpose of creating a sonic environment conducive to meditation and also one that generates aspects of a spiritual geography.

++++

According to the museum's press release, Ray Kass, the
founder and director of the Mountain Lake Workshop, invited Cage
there to paint, and they began a series of collaborative experiments
with watercolor pigments. As Cage experimented with watercolor
for the first time, he used paper towels as test sheets to acquaint
himself with the new medium. Kass viewed these beautiful studies
as more than just test sheets and encouraged Cage to make an
artwork with them. Cage then invited Kass to make a piece with
them. Twenty years later, Kass, along with Dr. Stephen Addiss,
returned to Kass' collection of Cage's archived paper towel
paintings, selecting works that reflect the Zen narrative of Ox-
Herding pictures, an illustrated parable for the path to and beyond
enlightenment that Cage often referred to in his writings.
Accompanying each of the images is a poetic fragment from Cage's
writings, selected by Addiss to further connect the images with the
ancient Zen parable. Addiss is a composer, musician, poet, painter
and historian of Japanese art. He studied with Cage in his now
famous classes in "Experimental Composition" at The New School
for Social Research, during which time Cage often talked about D.T.
Suzuki, with whom he had studied Zen.

Cage often used the *I-Ching*, also known as the *Book of
Changes*, and dates back to 3rd to the 2nd millennium BC, as a
source for determining the direction to take in his composition and
visual work. For example, in the book that accompanies the

exhibition, *John Cage: Zen Ox-Herding Pictures*, Ray Kass writes about when he presented Cage with a set up for producing a set of watercolor paintings based on smooth rocks in the New River, nearby the Mountain Lake Workshop, and perhaps inspired by Cage's own interest in the fifteen stones of the Zen-inspired Ryōanji garden in Kyoto, Japan, which is considered one of the finest examples of a *kare-sansui*, or Japanese rock garden.

I invited him to experiment in making watercolor paintings using the stones that he had selected the previous day. He was silent for a few moments while he looked over the arrangement of the materials that I had prepared. He then took out a folder containing a computer printout of random numbers based on the hexagrams of the "I-Ching" and immediately set to work making a program for a painting.

During the process of making these works, Cage would test his brushes on brown paper towels. Kass' was intuitive enough at the time to see something special in them. He writes, "At one point I suggested that we do something with the collection, and Cage said that *I* should *make a piece out of them.*"

In other words, Cage did not set out to consider his paper towel test sheets as responses to the Ox-Herding poems, nor did he generate the poems to accompany the test sheets. Although executed after his death, they have been done with Cage's implicit blessing and earlier instruction to Kass that he "make a piece out of them."

The idea that others could participate in the making and

remaking of Cage's work is essential to Zen thought in which subject and object collapse. In this manner, life's struggles lessen as one embraces that which is out of one's control. In Los Angeles, Cage's process was perhaps most evident, in regard to visual art, in the posthumous 1993 exhibition at The Museum of Contemporary Art, *Rolywholyover A Circus*. For example, in one of the galleries there were storage racks that contained a variety of works by almost 150 artists. Cage had instructed that the display of the art on the racks being changed daily by gallery attendants, based on the I-Ching.

Taking a cue from John Cage, and his willingness and encouragement to embrace that which is out of one's control as part of one's creative process, I've decided to recontextualize excerpts from the manual that accompanies my air conditioning unit (an apparatus that is dominant in my life at the moment during these hot months of Cage's centenary celebrations) by juxtaposing them with translations of the Ox-Herding poems, which are posted in the exhibition, that served as an ongoing inspiration to John Cage. I consider my reconceptualization to be in alignment with how this exhibition came together. Oddly, I feel that, even though the operating manual is written in a neutral manner, there is a subtext of a narrative about the struggle to control one's environment. This is true literally in that the goal of the manual is to instruct one on the best and effective manner for cooling the air in the house but, through juxtaposition with an ancient narrative about the struggle to control one's desires, fears, and ego, it also seems to be a metaphorical tale about the impossibility of maintaining control. Perhaps I will start a side business—Cage's HVAC Service, where we say, "Forced Air Is Music to Our Ears!"

++++

An Operating Manual for Air Conditioner and Ox-Herding Poems

By Tyler Stallings in unintended collaboration with poet C'hing-chu and York Heating & Air Conditioning

Key

The Ox-Herding Poems represent a spiritual journey that represents a search for one's true self that begins with a journey outward but then enlightenment is found through a journey inward, yet returns to the world with a new viewpoint of compassion for everyone and everything.

According to a didactic panel in the exhibition, the earliest series of Zen ox-herding poems was written in China around 1050 by C'hing-chu. The series that became the best known was written and illustrated by K'uo-an Shihyuan in the mid-twelfth century. His pupil Tz'u-yuan published these paintings and poems as woodblock prints. Translations of K'uoan's poems are provided by Stanley Lombardo, and are in italics.

I've written nutshell interpretations in the parentheses next to each heading.

Lastly, an excerpt from the air conditioning manual follows the poem. The paragraphs are in the same order found in the manual, as if they represented not only a journey of maintenance of hardware but of the spirit too. They have been edited slightly.

1. **Searching for the Ox** (aimless searching; the ox has been there waiting to be seen again)

Searching through tall, endless grass
Rivers, mountain ranges, the path trails off.
Weary, exhausted, no place left to hunt:
Maples rustle, evening, the cicada's song.

This high efficiency air conditioning system has been precision engineered, manufactured of high quality materials, and passed many rigorous tests and inspections to ensure years of satisfactory service. That's why you can rely on efficient, trouble-free operation.

2. **Finding its Traces** (beginning a path towards enlightenment)

Along the river, under trees—jumbled tracks?
Thick fragrant woods, is this the way?
Though the ox wanders far in the hills
His nose touches the sky. He cannot hide.

Your system is fully automatic. Set the thermostat and forget it. And it's automatically protected from damage by voltage fluctuations or excessive heating or cooling demands.

3. **Seeing the Ox** (perceiving the everyday as a source of realization)

Oriole on a branch chirps and chirps,
Sun warm, breeze through the willows.
There is the ox, cornered, alone.
That head, the horns! Who could paint them?

If your hand is wet and you blow on it, it feels cool because some of the moisture is evaporating and becoming a vapor. This process requires heat. The heat is being taken from your hand, so your hand feels cool. That's what happens with an air conditioner.

4. **Catching the Ox** (discipline is required to break old habits)

Last desperate effort, got him!
Hard to control, powerful and wild
The ox sprints up a hill and at the top
Disappears into the misty clouds.

Your thermostat puts full control of the comfort level in your home at your fingertips. DO NOT switch your thermostat rapidly "On"

and "Off" or between "Heat" to "Cool." This could damage your
equipment. Always allow at least five minutes between changes.

5. **Taming the Ox** (believe in your path and stop deluding yourself
with too much doubt)

Don't lose the whip, hold on to the rope
Or he'll buck away into the dirt.
Herded well, in perfect harmony
He'll follow along without any constraint.

Although thermostats may vary widely in appearance, they are all
designed to perform the same basic function: to control the
operation of your air conditioning or heat pump system. Regardless
of size or shape, each thermostat will feature a temperature
indicator; a dial, arm, or push button for selection of the desired
temperature; a fan switch to choose the indoor fan operation; and a
comfort switch for you to select the system mode of operation.

6. **Riding the Ox Home** (joy is less struggle)

Riding the ox home, taking it easy,
The flute's notes vanish in the evening haze.
Tapping time to a folksong, happy as can be—
It's all too much for words.

The computerized electronic thermostat is actually a sophisticated electronic version of a manual changeover type. This thermostat includes features that allow "set-back" temperature variations for periods of sleep, or while you are away during the day, and means energy savings for you.

7. **Forgetting the Ox** (stillness and oneness with the ox, the self, and the world)

Reaching home on the back of the ox,
Rest now, the ox forgotten.
Taking a nap under the noon sun,
Whip and rope abandoned behind the hut.

The main power to the system must be kept "ON" at all times to prevent damage to the outdoor unit compressor. If necessary, the thermostat control switch should be used to turn the system "OFF". Should the main power be disconnected or interrupted for eight hours or longer, DO NOT attempt to start the system for eight hours after the power has been restored to the outdoor unit.

8. **Transcending the Ox** (emptiness and a lack of delusions allows openness to the world)

Whip, rope, self, ox—no traces left.
Thoughts cannot penetrate the vast blue sky,
Snowflakes cannot survive a red-hot stove.

Arriving here, meet the ancient teachers.

For the most efficient operation, keep storm windows and doors closed all year long. They not only help insulate against heat and cold, but they also keep out dirt, pollen, and noise. Closing drapes at night, keeping fireplace dampers closed when not in use, and running exhaust fans only when necessary will help you to retain the air you have already paid to heat. Keep lamps, televisions, or other heat producing sources away from the thermostat. The thermostat will sense this extra heat and will not be able to maintain the inside temperature to the desired comfort level.

9. **Returning to the Source** (view the world with serenity by not imposing one's will so much)

Return to the source, no more effort,
Just staying at home, sitting in the hut,
Blind and deaf to the world outside.
The river runs by itself, flowers are red.

With the comfort control switch in the "COOL" position, the system will operate as follows: When the indoor temperature rises above the level indicated by the temperature adjustment setting, the system will start. The outdoor unit will operate and the indoor fan will circulate cool, filtered air. When the room temperature is lowered to the setting selected, the system will shut off.

10. **Entering the Marketplace** (spread the good will of your enlightenment by returning to the world as an example)

Barefoot and shirtless, enter the market
Smiling through all the dirt and grime.
No immortal powers, no secret spells,
Just teach the withered trees to bloom.

A periodic inspection, cleaning, lubrication, and adjustment of your heat pump are available from your dealer. Be sure to ask him about this service.⍰For those who prefer to do-it-yourself, follow the instructions to care for your system. ☐

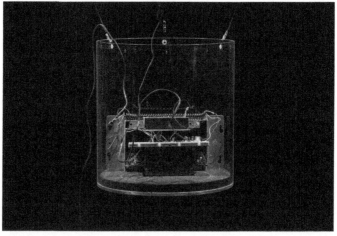

Area 51: A Sound Installation by Venzha Christ

(2013)

Area 51: A Sound Installation by Venzha Christ is a new site-specific, sound installation at UCR ARTSblock's Culver Center of the Arts. It is based on the artist's travels to the secretive U.S. military base, Area 51, also known as Dreamland, or Groom Lake, where he made recordings of the sounds emanating from and around the base. Located in the southern portion of Nevada, the base's purpose has never been announced officially. In fact, the U.S. Federal government has acknowledged its existence only recently. However, it has been assumed that it is used to develop experimental aircraft and weapons. UFO sightings are frequent in the area. But, because of the secrecy around the base, it is hard to verify whether that unusual shape in the sky represents extraterrestrial, aerodynamic engineering, or U.S. technology to evade radar when crossing covertly into foreign lands.

It is these secrets and ambiguities that Venzha explores in this new work created especially for UCR Culver Center of the Arts Black Box intermedia studio. Venzha is a sound artist based in Indonesia who has been invited by University of California, Riverside's Music Department for a month-long residency, which includes creating the installation at UCR's Culver Center of the Arts.

Venzha Christ is from Yogyakarta, Indonesia. He is a prolific artist, initiator, and leader in media and art and science research. Focusing on media art since 1999, he created the HONF Foundation with the goal of fusing education, art and technology with local communities. He has produced and organized many projects such as public art installation, media performance, media art festival, technology and science research, video work festival, workshops, discussion, DIY gathering, electronic and media culture movements. Venzha is founder of HONF lab, electrocore sound project, C.O.S (Circle Of Satan), v.u.f.o.c lab, Micronation / Macronation project, etc. He is director of YIVF (Yogyakarta International Videowork Festival) and CELLSBUTTON (Yogyakarta International Media Art Festival), which has been produced annually and organized by HONF since 2005.

Historically, Venzha's use of "field recordings" to record ambient, often low-level sounds out in the environment, using highly sensitive equipment, can be traced to Futurism's and Dada's interest in sound, to musicologist John Lomax traveling the country to record folk music *in situ*, to Frenchman Pierre Schaeffer's development of musique concrète in the1940s, and many others up to the present, such as the esteemed Pasadena-based sound artist (and painter), Steve Roden.

The device used by Venzha around Area 51 was an ultrasonic frequency receiver. According to René T.A. Lysloff, the co-curator of the exhibition and UCR associate professor in the Music Department, it is able to receive sounds that we normally cannot perceive (frequencies above about 20 KHz). The device automatically converts these sounds to lower frequencies perceptible to humans. Every second of every day, we are bombarded with such sounds, many emanating from electricity and the electrical components we use while others reach earth from space. These sounds bounce around our environment, sometimes absorbed by certain objects and landscapes but more often they are reflected—even amplified—by buildings and other large hard objects. Thus, the ultrasonic frequencies soundscape of any given location is unique and may change radically over a short time. Near Area 51, Venzha recorded the sounds his device was able to pick up (and convert to audible sound) and, along with radio frequencies (from Short Wave to Long Wave) as well as ambient sounds, used them as part of his installation project at the Culver Center. Two of Venzha's devices are displayed in the installation.

During his residency, Venzha also traveled out to the Joshua Area to visit The Integratron. Originally, it was a building constructed by George Van Tassel, and was done so, purportedly, with plans provided by Venusians. It was meant for rejuvenation and time travel. After Van Tassel's death in 1978, a variety of people owned the building. The present day owners now promote The Integratron as an "acoustically perfect structure." The building is currently open at select times and includes regularly performed "sound baths."

As a side note, Victoria Vesna, an artist interested in the intersections of science and art and professor at UCLA, did an amazing project there in 2008: *BLUE MORPH*. It was an interactive installation that used nanoscale images and sounds derived from the metamorphosis of a caterpillar into a butterfly. It was represented at UC Irvine's Beall Center of the Arts in 2012 for a retrospective of her work, *MORPHONANO: Works by Victoria Vesna*. In Venzha's *Area 51* installation, the gallery is nearly pitch dark, so your eyes are useless at first, until your pupils adjust. However, sound vibrations from surround sound speakers touch your body, compelling you to enter. There are six skylights letting a little daylight. But, upon closer inspection, they are flat screen video monitors actually, hanging facedown from the ceiling. Their blue glows suggest views of the sky; some do contain views of an azure sky, as if to point to our preoccupation of viewing the world through screens. Others contain scenes of driving through the Nevada landscape around Area 51. Perhaps Venzha is suggesting that we live in a topsy-turvy world where the land has become sky and night sky is the ground upon which we stand now.

There are two circular, Plexiglas containers hanging from the ceiling at the center of the gallery, which are lit with spots. They are visual beacons that draw you into the gallery further. Once nearby, you can see that there is a customized, electronic board sitting inside each. Headphones are connected to them through which subsonic frequencies in Area 51 can be heard.

This experience in the gallery, along with the background of knowing about Venzha's visits to both Area 51 and The Integratron, demonstrates his desire to interact with the nearly imperceptible and the invisible in the form of sound. His approach is one that does bring our attention to that which envelops us: strange resonances, the secrecy of governments, and a desire for cosmic connections—all are masked from our eyes, but present when we open our ears. □

Part III

Desert Architectonics

Pump Up the Realism: Todd Brainard's Paintings

(2002)

Todd Brainard's kinfolk are ones who have not visited Los Angeles in a while—the photorealists. His estranged, largely east coast, relatives, who came to prominence in the mid-1960s, include Malcolm Morley, Chuck Close, Richard Estes, Audrey Flack, Robert Bechtle, Robert Cottingham, Richard McLean, and Don Eddy. Back then, they strained to reproduce a photograph precisely in paint, including the distortions of focus in the details of the original photograph.

Their works focused on scenes with shiny reflections in order to display prominently their craftsmanship, and perhaps as a teasing joke on past luminist landscapes, stressed neon lights aglow instead of the setting sun. But their work was claustrophobic in this all-over effect of glassy reflections. Building on a viewer's awe over such painterly skill, Brainard's approach to photorealism is much more conceptual and subtle.

He selects one element in his desert, urban landscapes to render in meticulous and sharply focused detail. It pops out from the surface, like a cheesy 3-D movie, but without the need for the cardboard goggles. Chosen elements include a cylindrical metal fence post as part of a yellow S-curve fence in *Northern Grade: road 33* or a yellow & black arrow directional sign in *Field 31*. Unlike the elements in the works of the earlier photorealists—shiny cars, light reflecting on plate glass windows, neon signage, glistening ceramics—that in reality and in reproduction were meant to seduce viewers, Brainard focuses on items, usually in the backdrop of a panoramic landscape, that are meant to limit ones movements in actuality: fences and signs.

He seduces the viewer to come in close and examine the focused clarity of the post or sign, but conceptually he keeps us at bay, for the rest of the image is slightly distorted, out of focus, and so we must decide if we are going to—jump over the fence or ignore the signage—and engage with the rest of the painting.

The settings in which the fences and signs are found poked into the earth are lonely sites, reinforced by the lack of people—an ugly dirt road, an observation platform overlooking a city in a valley, or a condo in a dry field accompanied by a solitary oil rig pumping crude from down deep. Brainard's emphasis on banal subjects suggests randomness in his decisions about the scenery to render, as if to make an implicit commentary on an empty culture. These haphazard and commonplace qualities are reinforced with titles like *Parcels 263, 264, 92, Section 19 (permit access)*, or *Observation Site #6*.

This approach to the California landscape fits within a long tradition that reaches back to painters in the earlier twentieth-century such Albert Bierstadt or Guy Rose who, like many painters in California, generated bucolic, sublime, god-found-in-nature scenes. They would reinforce the concept of a pristine wilderness by often eliminating any signs of the human touch. This is as opposed to the east painters who, in the past and to this day, recognized and depicted the contemplated entanglements between people and the environment.

Brainard melds the two. He presents us with open, glowing skies, reminiscent of luminist painters, but where sky meets earth, the artifacts of man's imposition on the landscape are evident. However, there is no human nor any living animal in sight, as if it were a post-apocalyptic scene, where germ warfare killed animals but left remaining, in a sarcastic gesture, the buildings standing for those who have no use for them—future generations of trees.

Oddly, this acknowledgment of a transformed landscape, pays homage to Robert Smithson, an unlikely connection to a conceptual and land artist. Specifically, the resonance comes from Smithson's illustrations made for his essay, *The Monuments of Passaic*, published in 1967. Smithson, like Brainard, also focused on details such as pavements, trenches, pipes, and roads, suggesting that they all have an esthetic potential. In this essay, and much of his artwork, Smithson's thread was his fascination with entropy and the enlightenment that it can provide once understood.

He, like Brainard, expressed multiple and contradictory roles for his work: nostalgia for uninterrupted nature, yet acknowledging that there has actually rarely been such a case, followed by a sense of loss over the landscape scarred with industrialization. But instead of making paintings of never-existent, idyllic landscapes, like Bierstadt or Thomas Cole, Smithson went with entropy. It is a concept that suggests that there are no cycles, that is, there is no possibility for a reoccurring past. Rather, there is only transformation from one state to another. So, whether it be in

Smithson's *Spiral Jetty*, that recycled a dead sea, but also contained the artwork's own destruction, as Smithson knew, when its lifeless water would eventually subsume his reclamation, or Brainard's depiction of the developed environment, neither mourn. Both suggest that it can once again be transformed, though that next level of existence is dependent on whether you decide to trespass.

Brainard also contradicts landscape tradition with the orientation of his wood panels. The longest side of the panel is not horizontal, in order to go with the logic of a panoramic horizon line. Rather, many of the works, such as *Proposed Tracts #872, 873*, are composed vertically. In this particular work, the perpendicularity is intensified by a diamond-shaped, bold red sign on a metal support that has been erected in the painting's foreground. It is almost life-size too, like many of the accentuated barriers and guideposts that inhabit his work, creating a participatory relationship with viewers, an association that *repopulates* the industrial landscape with real people, though they breathe beyond the edges of the painting only.

Additionally, the verticality in combination with the wood panel support references architecture—even the very room in which they hang—more than the organic landscape, reinforcing Brainard's exploration of artifice—the meaty subject for any painter. The boldness of the colors in his work, which emphasize shape over line, along with the cool and smooth application of the paint, erasing the hand of the painter, suggests that they are signs themselves to be read from across a living room, or from a car passing in front of the gallery windows, like a billboard. Similar to James Rosenquist's work, they announce nothing specific, sans any text, but just inject an ambiguous image of a landscape into the real landscape.

However, once we park the car or put down our drink to walk across the room, and take a closer look, all these interpretations of social conscience form more a backdrop to Brainard being a dexterous landscape painter. He is obviously fascinated by the ability of one millimeter of paint on a two-inch wood support to suggest a hundred miles in the distance. He delights in the artifice of painted illusions.

Brainard does provide us with a sophisticated and crafty visual pun that indicates his complicated hobnobbing of photorealism, California landscape painting, Romanticism, Pop art, conceptualism, land art, and environmentalism: if you compare the works, you will discover what feels like a preponderance of oil wells, and then you will recall that what you are viewing is indeed *oil* paint. □

Laurie Brown: Recent Terrains

(2001)

Recent Terrains is an exhibition of Laurie Brown's panoramic landscape photographs taken between 1991 and 1998. Her work reveals the inseparability of nature and culture in late twentieth and early twenty-first century America. Her subject matter is the Orange County landscape in transition, returning often to its newest cities, such as Laguna Hills, Aliso Viejo, and Rancho Santa Margarita. Brown records a mediated landscape in which nature is a drawing board upon which mankind's actions can be seen very clearly.

For the past twenty-five years, Brown has utilized the panoramic format almost exclusively. In the late nineteenth century, approximately fifty years after photography was invented in 1839, this format was utilized to capture the vastness of the American west that was the nation's newly acquired territory. In Brown's work, the panorama encourages the eye of the viewer to roam across its surface from one end to the other, just like a land developer surveying "undeveloped" land from atop his perch. Or in a more cosmic sense, the panorama helps situate the changing landscape of Orange County in a larger context—the planet and human history. By stepping back we can see it in the bigger perspective, literally and figuratively.

Brown's exploration of our complicated relationship with the land focuses on the usual debate of "natural" versus "artificial."

However, she does not take sides, rather she points to the interdependent relationship between the two. She suggests that being presented with an either/or set of options has been the wrong approach for too long. This interest is connected to the investigations of the monumental earthwork artists such as Robert Smithson and Michael Heizer who moved tons of earth and rock in the deserts of the American West to create massive earth sculptures sometimes reminiscent of ancient burial mounds/sites, such as Smithson's 1970 *Spiral Jetty*, a 1,500-foot-long rock-and-salt-crystal jetty in the Great Salt Lake of Utah.

Like Smithson, Brown's work, possesses an air of indifference, coming to the defense of neither the environmentalist nor the developer. She is not an idealistic artist who retreats only to the picturesque, ignoring the concrete around her, or only seeing the landscape in terms of some past glory when man and God were bound together. Rather, she is an artist who creates work that is meant to suggest that there has been and will always be an intense relationship between nature and people. In this same radical light, Smithson wrote in the 1970s that "art can become a resource that mediates between the ecologist and the industrialist.... Such devastated places as strip-mines could be re-cycled in terms of earth art. The artist and the miner must become conscious of themselves as natural agents." Similarly, Brown refuses to create a hierarchy in which she places nature above civilization. Her work does not represent the romanticism of cascading waterfalls and ruggedly jagged snow capped mountains. These images constitute a still prevalent vision, one popularized by Ansel Adams, for example, in which the wilderness is depicted as a site of spiritual redemption.

Brown's work is also connected to several photographers, such as Robert Adams, Lewis Baltz, and Bernd and Hilda Becher, who were exhibited together in the 1975 groundbreaking exhibition, *New Topographics: Photographs of a Man-Altered Landscape.* Their photographs were usually bereft of people, as are Brown's, yet focused on the signs of the human, such as malls, tract houses, and industrial parks. Often these sites were shown in their larger context, with a mountain in the background or in the surrounding desert where they had been seemingly plopped down. It is left to the viewer to decide if the photographs depict images of progress or of civilization's downward spiral.

In Brown's photographs, we see that the earth has been moved, but we do not see the machinery that has moved it. In some photographs we do see houses and we do see the tread marks of a tractor in the dirt. As an observer on the scene, the landscapes appear like the familiar photographs of the moon's surface, or of the aftermath of a neutron bomb—where the people are killed but the buildings still stand.

However, this glum feeling is counterbalanced by the beauty of the starkness in Brown's black and white, gelatin silver prints. There is a serenity that discounts any sense of judgment on the part of Brown. She leaves it up to the viewer to decide if it is good or bad that the land seems so mutable. Her territory is the space between what is being done in preparation and what is to come later. It is a moment of arrested development allowing for a quietness in the images that suggests both mankind's reverence for the land and our reliance upon it, for better or for worse.

A motif in Brown's photographs is the graded hillside. Photographed before they have been adorned with vegetation and built upon, they appear like ancient Mayan or Aztec stepped pyramids. In some photos, at the base of these temple mounts, there is an assortment of boulders arranged in a rough circle. The combination of the earthen pyramids and rock circles suggest sites of ancient but still practiced rituals. In reality they are just the evidence of a landscape in transition, preparing the site for development.

This connection between time and place has been a recurring theme in Brown's work. She made this most clear in her *Divining Western Waters* series, also included in the exhibition. She constructs the images for these prints by overlapping photographs from both the early and the late twentieth century. Each print includes a stereographic image made in the early 1900s and a panorama of a contemporary landscape and depicts a contemporary relationship with waterways, such as the concrete basin of Lake Matthews in Riverside County.

In the older stereographs, the West has been reduced in scale, thus allowing a viewer in the early twentieth century to have had a vicarious experience of the wilderness while sitting in the comfort of their living room, just like going to the movies of today. But then Brown expands back out the scale of time and place, at least conceptually, by juxtaposing it with a contemporary landscape. It is a strategy that calls for the viewer's participation rather than their passive gaze.

The simultaneous presentation of the two images suspends the viewer between two time periods. Brown presents us with two frames of reference literally. The frame of the stereograph from the 1920s within the frame of the contemporary photograph. The two frames of reference suggest seamlessness between past and present, posing the questions: what are the differences and what are the similarities?

Despite Brown's focus on the changing landscape, especially through housing development, she is less political than she is anthropological with her intentions. Her work is a cross between the panoramas of nineteenth-century geological survey photography and the recording of earth sculptures in progress. She does not retreat from urban encroachment but attempts to find another kind of significance within it for herself. Essentially, her strategy is to reorient our understanding of the landscape, to make us see that, whether we like it or not, its future is tied to human desire. She does this by showing the beauty of a stark landscape that rests between nature and artifice, between aesthetics and politics, and between a romantic pastoral and an ironic beauty. □

Cabins in the Desert: Ruminating on Kim Stringfellow's Exploration of Jackrabbit Homesteads

(2013)

Jackrabbit Homestead: Tracing the Small Tract Act in the Southern California Landscape, 1938-2008, a project by Kim Stringfellow explores the cultural legacy of the Small Tract Act in Southern California's Morongo Basin region near Joshua Tree National Park. "Beyond the proliferation of big box chains, car dealerships, fast food joints, and the nameless sprawl located along California State Highway 62 the desert opens up," as Stringfellow states in her book, whose title the exhibition adopted as its own. She goes on to write that "out there, just past Twentynine Palms, in an area called Wonder Valley, where signs of familiar habitation seem to fade from view, a variance appears in the landscape in the form of small, dusty cabins—mostly abandoned—scattered across the landscape. The curious presence of these structures indicates that you are entering one of the remaining communities of 'jackrabbit' homesteads left in the American West."

Stringfellow's detailed research about the history of the Small Tract Act can be found in the book. This exhibition consists of photographs, research materials, a web-based, multi-media presentation that features a downloadable car audio tour, and a to-scale layout in black tape on the gallery floor of one of the 400-square foot cabin floor plans called "The Nugget."

The mostly derelict homesteader cabins are the remaining physical evidence of former occupants who were some of the last to receive land from Uncle Sam for a nominal fee through the Small Tract Act of 1938. It was established when Pasadena-based Dr. Luckie suggested that World War I veterans, who were affected by poison gases during the conflict, for example, relocate to an arid climate for their health. However, it was not until the 1950s, after World War II, when there was a real land rush for the Small Tracts. People wanted to escape growing cities and their problems and, perhaps, wanted to experience one of the American, mythological dreams of "going West." After all, it was in the 1950s, when both western films and novels were at the height of their popularity, exemplified by television with the series *Bonanza*, by John Wayne films, and Louis L'Amour's novels. These notions lent themselves to the Small Tract boosters too, especially by local municipalities that were motivated to increase homeowners in order to add to their tax base (a familiar story that continues to this day throughout the U.S.).

It was these abandoned structures that Stringfellow noted along Highway 62, north of Joshua Tree National Park, while driving through on vacations and doing projects around the Salton Sea area. She moved into a Joshua Tree (JT) home eventually, though not a jackrabbit homestead. Like the mid-century homesteaders, she was attracted by the solitude of the desert but, as an artist, she was also interested in being closer to a source of fascination for her: the built environment in arid regions.

She began to look into the history of the cabins, but discovered that a detailed account of the Small Tract Act was not evident. *Desert Magazine* would prove to be an invaluable resource, as it was one of the Act's original boosters, and is published still out of Palm Springs. She found, for example, that the Twentynine Palms Historical Society focused mainly on early homesteading from the 1860s to the 1920s when big tracts were dispersed by the federal government for agriculture or mining. In fact, there were once budding fields in the Eastern Mojave region in the early twentieth century, according to Stringfellow, but it was during an anomalous wet period. Nonetheless, despite the short time frame of optimal weather conditions, it provided fuel for the boosters to attract newcomers to a desert Eden in the West.

Subsequent to her research in the library stacks, she spent a year and a half in the field documenting the homestead cabins in Wonder Valley primarily. Many others had been destroyed by San Bernardino County that raised many of the cabins in the late 1990s and early 2000s. She mapped the cabins methodically by matching her GPS coordinates of cabins she found with the Bureau of Land Management's (BLM) online database of Small Tract Act plot maps. An aspect of their roadside attraction is a combination of the cabins being somewhat identical in size since most owners only cared to meet the minimal 400 square feet required for a structure to prove up the land, along with being placed at the center of their five-acre plots, for the most part. In other words, their seeming equidistance from one another suggests detailed planning, but as to why it would be done to such a degree in a desolate area would appear to be a mystery. But, of course, the answer comes from the BLM's steadfast method of overlaying a grid rectangles atop the landscape in order to "manage it," regardless of the terrain.

Many of the cabins were abandoned despite the ease of owning a piece of the West at less than $200 (as there were fees involved). This response by their owners was due in part to the unexpected harshness of the desert and the lack of infrastructure that the counties were not interested in building to service the tracts, such as water, power, sewers, and roads. It was not until the 1950s and 60s that electricity was installed in some areas, although water still came from either drilling a well or having it delivered by truck. The original owners, or their inheritors, just left the structures to the elements then. Today, all that remains sometimes is the original concrete pad, which adds even more mystery for trekkers who come upon them, uninformed about the history of the area.

The abandoned cabins were like time capsules for Stringfellow. She was trespassing, technically, but then who was there to even notice. She would find, to her surprise, that domestic items, such as beds, tables, and dressers, were still present from the 1950s and 1960s, as if the occupants had left suddenly. Such scenes feed an apocalyptic imaginary in our culture; a pervading theme today in so many science fiction films, television series, and video games.

Lately, there has been a burgeoning movement of visual artists relocating to JT and the surrounding area along Highway 62 for the past ten to fifteen years. Several have obtained a homesteader cabin as part of their new beginning; due in part to affordability, along with being inspired by their unique regional history.

Their relocation is akin to the spirit of the Wild West— seeking to redefine oneself, access spiritual renewal, and perhaps discover a kind of utopia. Artist Andrea Zittel's establishment of *A-Z West* perhaps best exemplifies the move, as does her subsequent creation of "High Desert Test Sites," an annual art happening. Prior to Zittel's move, Noah Purifoy, an important Los Angeles installation artist, who co-founded Watts Tower Art Center in the 1960's, moved to the desert in 1989, and created a nearly three-acre, indescribable sculpture garden made from human detritus.

Stephanie Smith, a design architect who has taught at downtown L.A.'s Southern California Institute of Architecture (SciArc), created Ecoshack in 2003. She was attracted to sustainable design and green lifestyles so she transformed a homesteader cabin into a green design lab. She was interested in "how a dwelling can be small, close to the landscape, and handmade, yet be effective," as she states in one of the audio tracks on Stringfellow's audio tour of cabins visible from Highway 62. It is a downloadable MP3 so that people can listen to it in their own cars, and also features Zittel's words too. In a kind of reversal of Buckminster Fuller's pioneering dome design, which aimed to use the least amount of materials to create the most amount of usable interior space, Smith's work suggests to me the use of the least amount of materials—in this case a historic 20 x 20 foot homesteader cabin—in order to have not the most interior livable space, but to make the least impact on the landscape and to respect its "bigness," whereby its "exterior" to the "interior" of the cabin becomes part of one's living space too. In essence, the sky then becomes one's "dome."

Perhaps part of the significance of Stringfellow's project is that 75 years later, in 2013, since the creation of the Small Tract Act in 1938, "smallness" has had resurgence with how to live. The inclination now is towards people living sustainably, lighter, freer, so that less land is occupied and abused. Perhaps there will be a new Wonder Valley land rush. Maybe readers will see new ads in *Desert Magazine,* which contain boosterish slogans that read, "Five acres! Your utopia!" □

From Beefcake to Skatecake: Shifting Depictions of Masculinity and the Backyard Swimming Pool in Southern California

(2011)

> "I came to Los Angeles for two reasons: The first was a photo by Julius Shulman of Case Study House #21, and the other was AMG's *Physique Pictorial*."[1]

—David Hockney

Most often, in mid-century architectural images of homes and pools, whether taken by Julius Shulman or by a staff photographer for any number of home-and-garden magazines, people are largely absent from the pool. The pool is clearly just an ornament to reflect the home's implied occupants—predictably, the family unit—either to enhance their glamour by way of its Hollywood associations, or to illustrate a rise in social status, as a newly minted consumer in the postwar era.

Although the dominant image of the backyard pool was as a backdrop for family values, privacy, and consumerism, there existed alternative uses and representations of the backyard pool as a site for expressing erotic desire, voyeurism, and a liminal state between nature and culture.

---

[1] David Hockney, *Bob's World: The Life and Boys of AMG's Bob Mizer*, ed. Dian Hanson (Köln, Germany: Taschen, 2009), 229.

Contrary to Shulman's often reproduced images of architecturally significant, clean-lined, modernist homes with placid backyard pools, such as the Kaufmann House in Palm Springs, this essay will look at photographs made between 1945 and 1980 that show men at play in backyard swimming pools. It will consider the work of two Los Angeles–based photographers: the beefcake photography of Bob Mizer and his peers from the 1940s–'60s published in his Physique Pictorial magazine, and Craig Stecyk's photo documentation of the DogTown Z-Boy skateboard team for *SkateBoarder* magazine in the 1970s. Each focuses on a redefinition of masculinity in relationship to the swimming pool towards a new vision embracing hedonism. This shift in values associated with the masculine—from a man as hardworking breadwinner for his family to the single, unattached, self-obsessed, and leisure-seeking man—accompanies a cultural shift from the early 1950s to the late 1970s from an economy based on production to one based on consumption.

"The introduction of the swimming pool as a pretext to show nude or seminude bodies was a spectacular opportunity," writes Thomas van Leeuwen in his groundbreaking book, *The Springboard in the Pond*, as "Eros could be shown in an athletic and hygienic context, providing legal as well as tasteful entertainment for the voyeur as a family man."[2] Here, van Leeuwen underscores the way the pool as family site provides cover for erotic desires that challenge mainstream modes of masculinity and domesticity.

---

[2] Thomas A. P. van Leeuwen, *The Springboard in the Pond: An Intimate History of the Swimming Pool* (Boston: MIT Press, 1998), 159.

Indeed, instead of creating images for families who may see their values reflected in magazines such as House Beautiful, or for the "family man," seeking out heteronormative, erotic images in men's magazines such as *Playboy*, both Mizer and Stecyk depict worlds of young men playing, posing, and emphasizing physique and performance. The work of each of these photographers was widely influential since their images were first published in magazines that could be found on most any magazine rack, as opposed to the rarefied setting of the fine art gallery or museum. However, decades after their first appearance in magazines, their works are now finding a place within these milieus.

Bob Mizer

Pioneer of gay, nude photography, Bob Mizer (1922–1992) founded the Athletic Model Guild, or AMG, in 1945. The business was located in his home, shared with his mother, located in downtown Los Angeles, and was formerly an old, rambling funeral parlor. After the photographer's death, Wayne E. Stanley, a friend and legal advisor, tended to his archives. In 2003 the company was sold to former physique photographer Dennis Bell, who continues to develop the brand and offers access to AMG archives through its website.[3] Mizer published *Physique Pictorial* for close to forty years, from 1951 to 1990.

---

[3] Athletic Model Guild website, http://www.athleticmodelguild.com, accessed February 24, 2011.

Mizer's photographs and those of other photographers whom he supported, and who sometimes shared the use of the same models, such as Bob Gentry, could be found printed both in his own magazine and in others published between the 1930s–60s that have been called "beefcake" magazines. While their primary market became gay men, until the 1960s these publications were typically presented as dedicated to encouraging fitness and health. They grew out of bodybuilding magazines that began publication in the early twentieth century. Up until several significant Supreme Court cases in the late 1960s, United States obscenity laws allowed women, but not men, to appear in various states of undress in images for publication.[4] After the U.S. Supreme Court lifted the ban

---

[4] Several significant cases in the 1960s brought about this shift in U.S. obscenity laws. H. Lynn Womack (1923-1985) was a headmaster of a boys' school in the 1940s and then a professor of philosophy at George Washington University. In 1952 he bought the small company Guild Press and, as publisher, editor, and distributor, turned it into a profitable gay publishing company with numerous affiliated enterprises. The United States Postal Service tried to stop the circulation of his publications Manual, Trim, and Grecian Guild Pictorial, but he took them to court and won the case on appeal in the Supreme Court in 1962. (See Guide to the H. Lynn Womack Papers, 1945–1994, Collection Number: 7441, Division of Rare and Manuscript Collections, Cornell University Library, http://rmc.library.cornell.edu/ead/htmldocs/RMM07441.html, accessed May 1, 2011.) Subsequently, Manual Enterprises Inc. v. J. Edward Day, 370 U.S. 478, was the first decision by the Supreme Court to hold that magazines consisting largely of photographs of nude or near-nude male models were not obscene under U.S. law, maintaining that "these portrayals of the male nude cannot fairly be regarded as more objectionable than many portrayals of the female nude that society tolerates." (See http://supreme.justia.com/us/370/478/ and http://uscode.house.gov/download/pls/18C71.txt; as well as Thomas Waugh, Hard To Imagine: Gay Male Eroticism in Photography and Film from Their Beginnings to Stonewall, New York: Columbia University Press, 1996.) Ultimately, the ban on full-frontal male nudity was entirely lifted on July 26,1967, when the U.S. District Court upheld "the right of all persons to receive materials dealing with the nude male figure" (U.S. v. Spinar and Germain, Decision, U.S. District Court, Minneapolis, Case 4–67 CR 15). In this pivotal case, Judge Earl R. Larson of the U.S. federal district court agreed with the prosecution that the intended market was a "deviant group," but to the amazement of the prosecution, he still found Spinar and Germain not guilty on all counts. Larson ruled that "the materials have no appeal to the prurient interests of the intended recipient deviant group; do not exceed the limits of candor tolerated by the contemporary national community; and are not utterly without redeeming social value." He even went further, acknowledging that these were gay magazines targeting a specifically gay market, and defending the rights of those consumers. "The rights of minorities expressed individually in sexual groups or otherwise must be respected. With increasing research and study, we will in the future come to a better understanding of ourselves, sexual deviants, and others." This victory in federal

on representing full frontal, male nudity in 1967, "the market was flooded with shots of every scrawny street kid willing to bare his all for a nickel bag."[5] Photographers such as Roy Dean, Lou Thomas, and Jim French were among a handful that maintained Mizer's aesthetic, one that was more admiring of the male physique than given to gratuitous display.

Like the Muscle Beach photos by Max Yavno found in museums and fine art books, beefcake magazines focused on presenting an abundance of photographs in each issue of brawny young men in sporty, fit poses. However, Yavno came out of a social-documentary aesthetic from the Photo League, a group with whom he associated in the 1930s when he was in New York, and thus was perhaps more concerned with the odd juxtapositions of personalities found at Venice beach, rather than a predilection for beautiful bodybuilder bodies.

Wayne Stanley, in his introduction to the recently published complete reprint of *Physique Pictorial*, characterizes Mizer in counter-distinction to Yavno:

Venice Beach provided Bob with the impetus to formulate the direction of his career, and by 1945 he was eager to earn his living as a professional photographer . . . As a result of his years at

district court was recognized at the time as a watershed moment, but today has been almost forgotten both by historians of pornography and obscenity and by historians of the gay movement. After this time, "the artistic, bodybuilding, and classical alibis that had been used to justify male nudity fell away. Within a year publications appeared with cover photos of naked men in bed, the sexual connotations no longer even thinly disguised." (David K. Johnson, "Physique Pioneers: The Politics of 1960s Gay Consumer Culture," Journal of Social History 43: 4 (Summer 2010): 867–892, accessed May 1, 2011, http://www.faqs.org/periodicals/201007/2069463751.html.)

[5] George E. Haggerty, ed. *Gay Histories and Cultures: An Encyclopedia* (New York: Garland Publishing, 2000), 342.

Venice Beach, Bob did not want for models after having turned AMG into a photographic studio. After a short while, handsome young men, in very large numbers, merely began appearing at the gates of AMG with the desire to be photographed. Manna from heaven![6]

What was groundbreaking about Mizer's work for *Physique Pictorial* was that he had no pretense about showing men without their clothes and celebrating their beauty. He was neither secretive nor apologetic. Historian, F. Valentine Hooven III, author of *Beefcake: The Muscle Magazines of America 1950-1970*, has called Bob's vision "unique at a time when there existed an enormous, untapped, and mostly closeted gay population hungering to see the beauty of the young male physique artistically photographed for its own sake."[7]

In the past ten years, Mizer's pioneering work has received increased recognition. This includes a feature film, *Beefcake*, that dramatizes events in his life, largely around a trial involving censorship of *Physique Pictorial*; exhibitions of his work in commercial galleries, such as Western Project in Culver City, California, and Exile Gallery in Berlin, Germany; reprinting facsimiles of every issue of *Physique Pictorial* in a three-volume set published by Taschen; and most recently the publication of Bob's World, also from Taschen, which focuses on Mizer's color

[6] Wayne E. Stanley, "Introduction," *The Complete Reprint of Physique Pictorial: 1951-1990*, 3 vols. (Köln, Germany: Taschen, 1997), 10–11.
[7] From an interview with Hooven included in Thom Fitzgerald, Director, *Beefcake*, 1998. Available from www.strandreleasing.com.

photography, and includes interviews with past associates, and biographical detail gleaned from Mizer's diaries.

Craig Stecyk

Craig Stecyk, Jeff Ho, and Skip Engblom opened the shop Jeff Ho Surfboards and Zephyr Productions on Main Street in Venice Beach in 1973. They developed a surfing team called the Z-Boys, who caught waves at Bay Street in Santa Monica and were infamous for adventurous surfing amidst the dilapidated pier-pilings of the Pacific Ocean amusement park, an area nicknamed "DogTown."

They were also passionate skateboarders, especially when the surf was down. Based on their surfing skills, they came to use banks of concrete throughout the city, especially at schoolyard playgrounds, to invent new, stylish moves. Instead of standing straight up, which had been the dominant stance, even in competition, they crouched low on their boards. It was a low-slung style, akin to a surfer guiding one's hand through a wave to steer their surfboard.

In the thirty years after the first issue of *Physique Pictorial*, Southern California had experienced rapid postwar suburban expansion, accompanied by the construction of a few hundred thousand, backyard swimming pools—made affordable and accessible through bank loans and cheaper building techniques. But in the 1970s in Los Angeles, a prolonged drought forced many homeowners to drain their pools. Word got around about these new "cement oases." The Z-Boys took their surf style of skating and their attitude of treating the urban landscape like their personal playground to the empty pools. In essence, Stecyk's photographs and the Z-Boys they depicted represented a draining of the Edenic California dream.

Stecyk wrote and photographed a series of innovative reports and interviews for *SkateBoarder* magazine that became known as the DogTown articles, which immortalized the Z-Boy lifestyle. His stories inspired a generation, and he is referred to as the godfather of the sport of skateboarding as it is known today. In the introduction to a collection of Stecyk's contributions to SkateBoarder magazine, editor Glen E. Friedman writes, "Virtually anyone who grew up during this period and knew *SkateBoarder* magazine as 'the Bible' has been influenced incredibly in his or her outlook and approach toward life and living by Stecyk's articles."[8]

Stecyk is one of the founders of *Juxtapoz* art magazine and has contributed to many different books. His life and that of the Z-Boys were portrayed in the 2001 award-winning documentary *DogTown and Z-Boys*, as well as the feature film *Lords of DogTown* in 2005.

In 2011, forty years after his initial skateboarding forays, Stecyk still embodies his peripatetic attitude and challenges notions of private property. This viewpoint is reflected in a recent interview with him, on the occasion of his work being included in Los Angeles' Museum of Contemporary Art's sprawling, historical

---

[8] C.R. Stecyk III and Glen E. Friedman, *DogTown—The Legend of the Z-Boys* (New York: Burning Flags Press, 2000), vii.

take on graffiti art since the 1970s, *Art in the Streets*, when he comments on the relationship between art and the urban landscape:

In this country we spend over $5 billion a year on graffiti abatement and prevention. It's strange to me. What's the difference between the Sistine Chapel and the side of an underpass? Not much. So why do we criminalize beauty?[9]

Similarly, although there is a dystopian aspect to a dry pool, it also invites trespassing, not only literally onto someone else's property, but also into the privacy and security of the nuclear family. Even though this notion suggests a provision for criminal acts, it also represents an act of rebellion against the traditional, rational-grid plan of cities. This urban layout can be found among many cultures going back centuries, but is perhaps best epitomized in the Western imagination by ancient Rome and its colonies, whose notion of the grid reflected the regimentation of its military camps. In this respect, as a tribe of men traversing Los Angeles's city streets, ending up in empty backyard pools, the Z-Boys came to break from this hegemony and embrace the irrational and nonlinear.

Magazines

The broad influence of the magazines in which Mizer and Stecyk published is evident by their circulation numbers. According

---

[9] Jori Finkel, "Street pioneers," *Los Angeles Times*, April 10, 2011, E1, 12.

to Hooven, by the mid-1950s, *Physique Pictorial* routinely sold over 40,000 copies. By 1978, *SkateBoarder* had one million readers.[10] The magazine images were units of exchange in the formation of varying forms of masculine identity around the country, whether gay, straight, beefcake, or "skatecake."

Mizer used campiness and subterfuge to play with identities in the 1950s and 1960s. Mizer's men were caught in a time of transition in which a new relationship between young men and consumption was developing. This was a change for the country as a whole that once based its economy on production rather than consumption. Stecyk and the Z-Boys embraced a new aesthetic of "looseness" that was in the air in the 1970s. In his book, *Getting Loose*, Sam Binkley defines looseness as "an affirmation of direct personal engagement as an active force in the fashioning of experiences, realized through a release of the self into the flow of natural impulses, desires and the sensuality and experience of everyday life."[11] In this spirit, the interaction between masculinity and consumerism in this period formed a new definition for a man—one who embraced pleasure and self-fulfillment.

The key to this whole process was the printed magazine. As Bill Osgerby writes in *Playboys in Paradise*, magazines were instrumental in "middle-class America's embrace of lifestyles increasingly at ease with a credo of pleasure, self-expression and

---

[10] Iain Borden, "Skateboarding and the Creation of Super-Architectural Space," *Body Architecture*, ed. Jonathan Hill (London and New York: Routledge, 1998), 201.
[11] Sam Binkley, *Getting Loose: Lifestyle Consumption in the 1970s* (Durham and London: Duke University Press, 2007), 2.

personal 'liberation' through consumption."[12] In *Playboy* magazine
for example, there was the occasional feature of the ideal bachelor
pad. In a plan from a 1962 issue, the editorial reads: "The
discerning city-dweller of individual ways and comfortable means
is turning more and more to the superb outlets for decorative and
architectural self-expression inherent in the town house. He is
beguiled by its intrinsic advantages of privacy and spaciousness
coupled with a metropolitan location just a shift of the gears away
from myriad urban attractions."[13] The accent is clearly on the single
man seeking privacy for self-satisfaction. As in many of the
bachelor pad designs published between 1956–70, the emphasis is
on the city dwelling too—the place of the man—rather than the
suburbs, the place of the woman, as it were. One might argue that
an unintended consequence is a blending of the two—an overlay of
feminized interior design onto the masculinized city grid. It
represents a new merging of the masculine with consumption, a
feature associated with the feminine in the not too distant past.

Writing about the changes of the 1970s as reflected in
men's magazines, Jonathan Rutherford writes:
The aspirant nuclear family of the 1950s began to fail to
reproduce a normative version of itself. The advent of a consumer
society combined with new permissive legislation on divorce and
sexuality challenged the styles of manliness and modes of power
necessary to reproduce and sustain traditional heterosexual

---

[12] Bill Osgerby, *Playboys in Paradise: Masculinity, Youth and Leisure-Style in Modern America*
(New York and Oxford: Berg, 2001), 3.
[13] R. Donald Jaye, "The Playboy Town House," *Playboy*, May 1962, 83-92, 102.

relations . . . Women's struggle for more independent lives meant that men began to negotiate their relationships with women and children on the basis of equality . . . the decade witnessed the emergence of trends which point toward the end not just of the nuclear family but of the family based on patriarchal domination.[14]

Moving past the 1970s, Rutherford quotes from a 1998 report by marketing consultants that explained to advertisers how best to represent today's "insecure man." They concluded that "'the most successful way to communicate with men in today's environment is to reflect the soul of primal man. Man the warrior, the hero. In a world where men find their most basic instincts thwarted, an advertiser who indulges their favourite [sic] fantasies should prosper.'"[15]

However, in a less cynical tone, one might view Mizer and Stecyk's depiction of men and their "primal," body-centered activities around the pool as examples of infusing a new hedonistic sensibility, one enhanced by being in the privacy of the backyard and around the liminal and libidinal swimming pool.

When one peruses all the issues of *Physique Pictorial* or looks at his films it is evident that Mizer created a safe zone within the high walls of his compound for his boys to relax and play. Once oiled up, they enacted scenes of jailor and convict, of Roman emperor and slave, of cop and perp, eventually ending in a fall-down orgy in which everyone gave in to the pleasure of their bodies, no matter

14 Jonathan Rutherford, "Preface," *Masculinity and Men's Lifestyle Magazines*, ed. Bethan Benwell (Oxford: Blackwell Publishing, 2003), 1.
15 Ibid, 2.

how many "laws" had been broken. At other times, the pictures simply showed the boys lounging, weightlifting, or stretching. What made it all work was that Mizer could get close. Unlike a studio set where there might be a lone artist with a model, or at most with some assistants looking on, Mizer created a crowd scene of boys in his backyard. It is as though he transported Muscle Beach to downtown L.A., and could enter the crowd when he wanted, as if he were a street photographer, or a cinéma vérité film director in his own backyard. All of this was done in an effort to not only keep hidden that which was against the law at the time,[16] but also to create an artificial environment that then becomes natural within the context of his compound.

In a similar vein, Stecyk was part of the team, so to speak, as a founder of the original surf shop from which the skateboarders arose. He hunted for the pools too. In many of his shots, you see his shadow in the frame. He was up close. Like Hunter S. Thompson, he wrote from a gonzo or New Journalism aesthetic in which he was both a reporter and a figure within the story too. Capturing the same uninhibited qualities that Mizer sought, Stecyk, writing in a 1975 SkateBoarder article about the high speeds and the "fourth-dimensional" experience of seeming weightlessness while surfing and skateboarding, he said in a most philosophical riff:

16 Dennis Bell at AMG writes that he was told by Wayne Stanley that the aerial photograph of Bob Mizer's compound, which accompanies this essay, and was reproduced prominently on the inside cover of the book *Bob's World*, was from helicopter police surveillance in the 1950s (email correspondence to author, April 12, 2011). Mizer obtained the photograph himself from the Los Angeles County Courthouse.

Pushing the old boundaries establishes the new "limits." In actuality, the only limiting factor is that of your imagination. You can go as far as you want to take it, or perhaps more aptly as far as it takes you. After you leave the realm of traditional preconceptions, you enter the area of endless freedom. There exists no right or wrong, rules are unheard of, and the course is uncharted.[17]

Stecyk's promotion of this type of "mobile, flexible and self-responsible self, unconstrained by tradition and collective obligation" is in line with the spirit of other sorts of lifestyle magazines in this period, which were influential in promoting an ethic of autonomous living.[18] *The Whole Earth Catalog*, published between 1968–72, perhaps best exemplifies this looseness of a melding with nature, and promoting independent living. As stated on the first page of each issue, its purpose was to counteract the failures of big government and big business.

In response to this dilemma and to these gains a realm of intimate, personal power is developing—power of the individual to conduct his own education, find his own inspiration, shape his own environment, and share his adventure with whoever is interested. Tools that aid this process are sought and promoted by *The Whole Earth Catalog*.[19]

Although it is a different guise from *Playboy*'s bachelor pad, these two publications share a focus on being self-made and self-expressive. One might argue that sports magazines and consumer-

[17] Craig Stecyk, "Fear of Flying: Speed, A Strange and Tragic Magic," *SkateBoarder*, Winter 1975.
[18] Binkley, Getting Loose, 6.
[19] Stewart Brand, *The Whole Earth Catalog* (Menlo Park, California: Whole Earth Catalog, 1968), 1.

oriented magazines for men, changed after 1967 and 1969. In 1967, obscenity laws against male nudity were lifted after several groundbreaking trials in the U.S. Supreme Court. And after the Stonewall riot in 1969, gays become more visible in society. These two elements combined began to change how men behaved, as well as how they were depicted and viewed by the mainstream.

Self-Reflexive Masculinity

It was these books and magazines in the 1960s–70s that provided guides and maps to the new loose lifestyle, acting as "a reflexive storying of the self."[20] When skateboarders photographed each other and circulated these images to their readers of the magazines they put into practice a self-reflexivity that redefined masculinity. Similarly, the argument applies to Mizer's magazine in which he encouraged men from all around the country to send in their own photos for publication in Physique Pictorial. Once published, they would see themselves in a new context that celebrated the male physique—their physique.

Bob's world is one of homoerotic playfulness. There is also the sense that through the playfulness, Bob is helping his young men learn to enjoy their bodies. In Craig's world of Z-Boy skateboarders, the underlying message is classic male bonding through the shared, extreme experiences of vertical leaps in empty pools and through the brigands' trespassing of private homes.

---

[20] Binkley, Getting Loose, 9.

Mizer's magazine represents a gay sensibility acutely aware of the codes of what represents a man in the 1950s and 60s. This self-reflexivity lies at the heart of the campiness in the images. There is an element of play in the photos and the films produced by AMG. The closed environment of the compound and the parodic nature of commenting upon traditional masculine roles perhaps enhance the friskiness.

In the erotically charged, coffee-table book *Bob's World*, John Sonsini, a contemporary portrait painter in Los Angeles and friend of Mizer who spent much time at Bob's compound in the late 1980s, reflects on the social atmosphere around the studio. He captures the sense of bonding through participating in an alternative life in the backyard in a pre-Stonewall era: "When you think of AMG being home, in many ways you could say Bob's films were elaborate home movies...."[21] This is evident especially in Mizer's short films. For example, in *The Booking Of A Hood*, a short five-minute, black-and-white film that would have been for sale through Physique Pictorial, you see a cop and his deputy, trying to arrest and jail a delinquent. Eventually, they all fall down into a wrestling match of oiled bodies. Today, it seems much less titillating and feels more like the project of an art student, armed with plenty of gender theory, attempting to be purposefully light about the physicality in an effort to say, "We're all human. We're all not only gay, but sexually polymorphous. It's not about who you are or what you look like, but about desire, touch, and imagination."

---

[21] John Sonsini, *Bob's World: The Life and Boys of AMG's Bob Mizer*, ed. Dian Hanson (Köln, Germany: Taschen, 2009), 121.

The spirit and outcome of this playfulness is described good naturedly by Mizer's associate David Hurles:

It has been written that AMG often had the feel of a summer camp, with Bob as the camp director. He placed value on traits, such as personality, that many of these men weren't aware could even have value. With Bob's help they easily opened themselves up, and in that process they became more than just pretty bodies, they became sexy and accessible.[22]

In this respect, over the course of the forty years that Mizer published the magazine, *Physique Pictorial* proved a reflexive articulation of masculinities and sexualities. Implicit in his poses is an examination of the construction, strengthening, and weakening of male media icons, as was the case with much gay porn from this time period. This is why one so often saw the clothes and accouterments of sailors, policemen, bikers, cowboys, and other representations of authority and traditional manliness, which could become a "costume" in which to "perform" when in the hands of a gay man.

In both cases, men were in taboo situations. For Bob, it was the ongoing harassment from the U.S. Post Office over obscenity— nude, male bodies in publications circulated by mail were not permitted. For the Z-Boys, they were defiantly trespassing on other people's property, and embracing a life of rebellious leisure rather than a work ethic, the fruits of which were the house and property that they invaded.

---

[22] David Hurles, "Tribute to Bob Mizer," *Outcome Magazine*, 1992, http://championstudios.net/amg/mizer1.htm, accessed February 24, 2011.

The notion of repetitive acts was central to these magazines' appeal; as Iain Borden writes, "this is a complex intersection of lived experience and mechanically reproduced imagery…the mechanical image projects the skater both back to themselves, and others."[23] And since actions were performed collectively, "the desire to enact the move and to have it reproduced is then the desire to be, at the same time, oneself, oneself as someone else, and all skaters in oneself."[24] The skaters become recognizable icons in the magazines.

Stecyk's Z-Boy skateboarders challenged the sports model of military-like discipline and bending the body to rational will. Rather, the Z-Boys were not he-men, but were putting themselves on display for one another. They enjoyed performing and watching one another's bodies in motion. They were aware that they were being photographed by Stecyk, and being written about, thus becoming new role models for young men around the country who would read SkateBoarder magazine.

This self-awareness is evident in at least two ways when one pages through *SkateBoarder*, paying close attention to the images of skaters in empty pools. Either they are looking directly at the camera, usually in a moment of bravado and sometimes self-mockery if they happen to be caught doing a bad trick, or they are flipping their board above the rim of the pool in order to show its underside. And there, one finds the DogTown logo, created by Stecyk himself, but usually hand drawn. The point is that they knew

---

[23] Borden, "Skateboarding," 211.
[24] Borden, "Skateboarding," 212.

that they were doing something different and wanted everyone to know it when they opened the pages of *SkateBoarder*, whether they were in Malibu, Phoenix, Atlanta, or Boston.

In a *SkateBoarder* article from 1979, Stecyk characterizes the DogTown lifestyle as it came to be known and publicized, "Traveling hundreds of miles, sneaking about in appropriate camouflage, employing hand-drawn maps, eluding security guards, and spending countless dollars and hours perfecting their art, the practitioners exude a fanatical dedication that eclipses the common definitions of total insanity. They are members of an elite group whose only membership requirement is that you attend the meetings...."[25] Here, he also evokes the sense of belonging and camaraderie central to this loose lifestyle.

In the context of the postwar backyard swimming pool, so often used as a location for shelter magazines to self-consciously display the nuclear family and its values, Mizer and Stecyk employ the same setting to pose a challenge to those values.

Architectural Space as Sensual Space

Mizer's and Stecyk's representations and actual use of the backyard pool are an example of architectural space rethought in terms of the body that occupies it. Both Mizer's boys cavorting and posing around the pool and Stecyk's skateboarders hugging the pool's empty curves emphasize a desire for one's body to be in

---

[25] Stecyk, *DogTown—The Legend of the Z-Boys*, 102. From an article published originally in *SkateBoarder* (February 1979).

motion. Their engagement with the architectural and social other represents a rebirth of body and identity.

Skateboarders work with centrifugal and centripetal forces on the body to create new moves within the bowl of the empty pool. Borden describes their use of the pool in facilitating their flowing actions as taking "on more the character of a prosthetic device, an extension of the body as a kind of fifth limb."[26]

Though only some of Mizer's published images depicted men posing in private, backyard swimming pools, the reality of the studio setting was that most of what was shot always centered on the pool. Clearly, Mizer recognized that the pool created a libidinal context for his boys to be in a constant state of undress, or readiness to be. Over the years, he purchased surrounding properties, expanding his compound and keeping his business behind closed doors.

Despite the compound's sprawling site, recognition of the pool's centrality is underscored by comments on building the set in a warehouse in Nova Scotia for Thom Fitzgerald's *Beefcake*, a film that blends dramatization of key events in Mizer's life along with documentary footage. Set designer D'Arcy Poultney noted:

Bob Mizer left an archive of about a million stills, as well as films made by his agency…. We knew what his house and studio looked like…. First thing we needed, of course, was a pool. We

---

[26] Borden, "Skateboarding," 204–205.

borrowed an above-the-ground pool and built Mizer's house and studio on two levels around the pool.[27]

The bowl shape of the pool, filled with water, with bodies suspended in it, cannot help but make one think of a baby in the womb. In this sense, both Mizer and Stecyk's images suggest a rethinking the role of the male, the husband, as a hardworking breadwinner. Rather, their men took pleasure in their bodies. They turned the architectural space of the pool into a transsexual site, as defined by Diane Agrest in her essay "Architecture from Without."[28] In it, she discusses how first-century architectural manuals written by the Roman Vitruvius, which were influential during the Renaissance, created a discourse in which a woman's place was "usurped by man who as the architect has the female attributes necessary for conception and reproduction."[29] Like the famous, fifteenth-century rendering by Leonardo da Vinci in which man's proportions determine those of buildings (which was based on and illustrative of Vitruvius's theories), Vitruvius called the naval, rather than the womb, both the symbol and literal source of creation; hence he saw man as at the center of creation rather than woman. Although Agrest's stance is critical, her notion of "architectural transsexuality" is adopted here in order to acknowledge the unique shape of the pool and its symbolism; in a

---

[27] William Norwich, "Beefcake: How Bob Mizer Pioneered Male Crotch-Shots," *The New York Observer*, October 10, 1999, http://www.observer.com/node/42079, accessed February 24, 2011.

[28] Diane Agrest, "Architecture from Without: Body, Logic and Sex," *Gender Space Architecture: An Interdisciplinary Introduction*, ed. Jane Rendell, Barbara Penner, Iain Borden (London and New York: Routledge, 2000), 358–370.

[29] Ibid, 363.

different light, Agrest's critique of architectural patriarchy is one that could be shared by Mizer and Stecyk.

In the case of Mizer and Stecyk, groups of men circulate around the womb-pool, both in its childbearing state, when it is full of water, and in its barren state, when it is drained of water. Their appropriation of this site in order to reconfigure and challenge dominant ideas of masculinity suggests an active process of rebirth. It is a representation in direct challenge to the single-family unit and the suburban identity of the backyard pool, where privacy and security separates and protects from homosexuals and trespassing skateboarders. Mizer and Stecyk, in their depictions of communal masculinity, suggest a space of shared experience, and in this sharing of an alternate value system find new security and renewal.

Backwards into the 1980s

It is appropriate that the period of time examined by *Pacific Standard Time*, a project developed as a partnership between the Getty Foundation and the Getty Research Institute, ends in 1980. For it was in the 1980s that there was a cultural jump backwards to the 1950s, as if World War II had just ended again, some thirty-five years later—the past is the future and the future is the past. The conservatism of the period managed to co-opt the energy of the liberatory self-reliance of the previous decades as "a countercultural emphasis on expressive self-realization and personal autonomy found an unlikely resonance with neoliberal visions of self-responsibility and enterprise."[30] In other words, privilege and consumer excess reared their heads again, in combination with moral restraint, obligation, and respecting so-called public norms.

Now, forty years after the drought of the 1970s, there is another sort of calamity stretching across the landscape of the Southland—foreclosures. The American dream of home ownership is disappearing with the Southern Californian dream of owning an oasis in the backyard along with it. As Stecyk says, "Today, there are more skateboarders than ever riding pools because of all the foreclosures. Fresno, the Inland Empire...many properties with good shapes. You used to find about pools by word of mouth, Nowadays, you have guys flying over foreclosed areas with helicopters searching for pools. You got real estate guys on the take to let you know when a property is empty and has a good pool."[31] This is a backyard *Shangri-La* regained for the primal man. Go forth, young man, and be photographed. Your body is the paradise. ☐

[30] Binkley, *Getting Loose*, 14.
[31] Craig Stecyk, interview with the author, October 9, 2010.

Part IV

Desert Planets

Free Enterprise: The Art of Citizen Space Exploration

(2013) (with Marko Peljhan)

Free Enterprise: The Art of Citizen Space Exploration is the first contemporary art exhibition in the U.S. to present an international array of artists and organizations who are exploring the potential democratization of space exploration and the intersection between artistic production and civilian space travel. The possibility of fulfilling the human dream to fly into space has been encouraged by a major political and cultural shift away from state-sponsored space activities—which are controlled by agencies such as NASA in the USA, JAXA in Japan and RKA in Russia — towards a private enterprise model.

Free Enterprise has been in the planning stages since fall 2009. Its presentation in 2013 arrives at a time when several private enterprise ventures have come to fruition. They include the successful launch in May 2012 of the *Falcon 9* vehicle and the *Dragon* space capsule by *Space X*, a company based in Hawthorne, California, which rendezvoused with the International Space Station; the soon-to-be-completed spaceport in New Mexico that will be the launch site for *Virgin Galactic's* space tourism program, and the burgeoning efforts of *XCOR Aerospace*, a Mojave based company represented in *Free Enterprise*. These developments are a clear sign that we are at a dawn of a new radical change in near-earth space exploration. Engaging artists directly in this discussion at an early stage is extremely important: it is the technology and capital that allow for exploration, but it is the imagination and the spiritual capital that create a new state of mind and allow for a broader awareness of humanity on Earth and beyond.

Background

Humankind has looked to the sky, stars, and planets for millennia. Empirical observations of celestial movements have influenced religious ceremonies, agricultural production, navigation of the oceans, and a reconsideration of Earth as the center of the solar system. Since the 1960s, humankind has explored our celestial neighborhood with landings on the Moon, Mars, Venus and Titan, walks in the vacuum of space, and habitation on the Skylab, Salyut, MIR space stations and since 1998 the International Space Station (ISS). With the Space Shuttle program and the world's first reusable spacecraft, we have gained a new sense of easy access to the cosmos since the 1980's.

The artists in *Free Enterprise* have intersected with these technological achievements. It has been their desire to go beyond the creation of metaphorical objects and events in order to be pioneering participants and citizens. Their spirit is akin to the days of the amateur, gentleman scientist, exemplified by Johannes Kepler, Isaac Newton, Benjamin Franklin, and Charles Darwin. However, since the twentieth-century, science has been led by pure research at universities and government laboratories, and by private labs that are both concerned with discovery and profit.

Today this research arena has expanded even further: public participation has increased through a variety of crowdsourcing citizen science ventures made possible by broad citizen access to technology. One of the early examples is the SETI screen saver distributed computing system in which private citizens could help with the search for extraterrestrial intelligence. A more recent one is Zooniverse, a citizen science web portal that includes numerous projects that allow users to participate in scientific research including classifying galaxies, collating climate data, discovering exoplanets, monitoring endangered species, and mapping the human genome.

Space is no longer a remote frontier. It is now within reach to build space-faring hardware with ready-made components. Participation in space research is now accessible to people who see themselves as citizens, amateurs, and—as exemplified by *Free Enterprise*—as artists.

The exhibition's structure of linking artists with the aerospace industry harkens back to the groundbreaking *Art & Technology* program at Los Angeles County Museum of Art in 1967-1971, almost the same time span as the flight years of the Apollo program. It paired artists with high technology and aerospace corporations of the time in the hope that new art forms might arise. The program was one of the milestones—with influence to this day—in probing the dense associations of art to technology and science.

Recent developments in the aerospace industry mark the dawn of a new space race. Space travel endeavors by private business and citizen initiatives represents a refocus from the cold war mentality of the 1960s in which space exploration was a grand, national assertion of collective identity, controlled by state ownership of the "final frontier." In contrast, our government now emphasizes private development of commercial sub-orbital flight and lunar exploration, signaling a shift from space as an abstract concept for state exploration into a de-regulated realm, unconstrained, and exposed to both socialization and capitalization. International artists are already exploring these untested territories with aerospace experts, engineers, scientists, visionaries and entrepreneurs.

The center of these businesses is in the American Southwest, particularly in Southern California, with most of the research conducted at the Mojave Air and Space Port near Edwards Air Force Base, about 115 miles north of Riverside. Other ventures are nested in the defense industry cluster in El Segundo, adjacent to Los Angeles International Airport and some in Silicon Valley. But for the last half of the 20th century, Southern California has been at the center of the world aerospace industry. Now, it is poised to achieve another status in very different societal and political conditions. The location of these enterprises in the American Southwest also embody complicated, newly resurrected questions related to westward expansion, the frontier spirit, and free enterprise versus government regulation. These new realities open up a Pandora's Box of discursive possibilities and vectors yet to be considered in the heady rush of technological/entrepreneurial adventure.

Although the private-public partnership is a somewhat novel model for space exploration, it is not new in the course of Western history. In fact, it has been the prime model for exploration and western expansion: the state sets goals and takes initial risks, followed by entrepreneurs, privateers or venture capitalists, who assume the ongoing burden of exploration. The legacy of this model is technological achievement, but one fraught with the exploitation and destruction of cultures and resources. It is exactly this schism on which *Free Enterprise* is focused, reflecting the current state of privately funded space exploration, and critically considering it from divergent perspectives, leaving room to explore utopian visionary roots where the arts and space collide.

Perhaps recognizing how fraught future space exploration may become, the *European Space Agency (ESA)* contracted in 2005 with *The Arts Catalyst* in London—an organization represented in *Free Enterprise*—to carry out a study of the "cultural utilization" of the *International Space Station (ISS)*, which included exploring artist residencies within the *Human Spaceflight, Microgravity and Exploration* directorate. In the report, *The Arts Catalyst* wrote that "one aspect of a cultural utilisation programme for the ISS could be thematic programmes, linking art-science-education-media. The environment is always a popular theme: the ozone layer, rising sea levels, changing weather systems, erosion of environment. Other themes might include orbital debris, meteors, Earth's magnetic field, and then more broadly solar system exploration, the ISS as a symbol of international cooperation, the nature/benefits of microgravity, the social issues of long-duration spaceflight, the nature of habitat in space, and more purely aesthetic explorations. The study team recommends that a network is developed that can link up artists with space science experiments at an early stage, soon after experiment selection. Such a network could incorporate workshops at ESA ground-based facilities, bringing together groups of artists and scientists, focused on particular areas of science."

Perhaps the most salient point made is the creation of an art-science network *at an early stage.* This recommendation is akin to the same issues with public art. Usually, the most interesting and successful work occurs when an artist is brought in early while architectural plans are in their planning stages and before construction begins. Similarly, the impetus for many of the artists in *Free Enterprise* is to be part of early integration with space exploration in order to make the best effort to keep the door open for not just private entrepreneurs, who may be more focused on a business model, but also for artists, who are focused on the larger cultural, ethical, and philosophical questions of what it means for humanity to reach beyond Earth.

Timeline of Work Represented

Free Enterprise is comprised of twenty-five artists, collectives, organizations, and initiatives, which includes several commissions for the exhibition and additions to the permanent collections at UCR ARTSblock: The Arts Catalyst (London, U.K.), Lowry Burgess (Pittsburgh, PA), Center for Land Use Interpretation (Culver City, CA), Richard Clar (Paris/Los Angeles), Skeith De Wine

(Santa Ana, CA), Kitsou Dubois (Paris), eteam (New York), European Space Agency Topical Team Arts and Science (international participants), Final Frontier Design (New York), Cultural Center of European Space Technologies / KSEVT (Vitanje, Slovenia), Agnes Meyer-Brandis (Berlin), MIR - Microgravity Interdisciplinary Research (international participants), Forrest Myers (New York), Trieste Constructivist Cabinet (Italy/Slovenia), Nejc Trošt (Slovenia/Houston, TX), Trevor Paglen (New York), Carrie Paterson (Los Angeles), Frank Pietronigro (San Francisco), Bradley Pitts (New York), Cosmokinetial Kabinet Noordung – Postgravityart (Ljubljana, Slovenia), Projekt Atol Flight Operations (Santa Barbara, CA and Ljubljana, Slovenia), Connie Samaras (Los Angeles), Christian Waldvogel (Zurich, Switzerland), Arthur Woods (Zurich, Switzerland), and XCOR Aerospace, Inc. (Mojave, CA).

The art represented in *Free Enterprise* includes work of early artistic pioneers. Here you will find work from the early twentieth-century: *Trieste Constructivist Cabinet* (Avgust Černigoj, Edvard Stepančič, Giorgio Carmelich and Josip Vlah), constructivists who envisioned an exhibition "ambient" with levitating sculptures in 1927—one of which has flown on the first arts-related parabolic flight in August 1999 and paved the way for the understanding of the meaning of non-gravitational spaces in the context of art. Another early flown space artwork is by Forrest Myers, the 1969 *Moon Museum*, a small, ceramic chip containing a variety of works by six artists including Andy Warhol and Robert Rauschenberg, that was sent up as an unauthorized, cultural, engineering and artistic "passenger" on the Apollo 12 lander.

Other artists including Lowry Burgess' project of mixing waters of the world for a project on the Space Shuttle with *Boundless Cubic Lunar Aperture*, Richard Clar's interspecies satellite project *Space Flight Dolphin*, and Arthur Woods' *Cosmic Dancer* sculptures aboard the Russian space station have been working since the early 1980s on space art projects and have flown them on the *Space Transportation System (a.k.a. Space Shuttle)* missions and on the *MIR* space station.

Also represented in *Free Enterprise* are the early explorations of choreography and dance in microgravity conditions by Kitsou Dubois in cooperation with the French space agency CNES and the first theatre performance with a public in a parabolic flight, the 1999 *Biomehanika Noordung*, which was staged by director Dragan Živadinov and his *Cosmokinetic Kabinet Noordung* in cooperation with *Projekt Atol Flight Operations* and the *Star City Gagarin Cosmonaut Training Center* with further development under the wider context of Postgravityart.

Subsequently, *Projekt Atol*, with artist Marko Peljhan, co-curator for *Free Enterprise*, and Rob La Frenais from *The Arts Catalyst*, together with the *V2 Institute for Unstable Media*, Leonardo Olats and the Multimedia Complex of Actual Arts started a series of parabolic flight campaigns under the heading of *MIR (Microgravity Interdisciplinary Research)* during which more than 30 artists and scientists took part in a series of flights from 2001 to 2008. Some of these are represented in *Free Enterprise*.

Other artists in *Free Enterprise* who benefited from their

efforts or arranged their own similar parabolic flights include
Agnes Meyer-Brandis' blend of mythology and science, and
Christian Waldvogel's success at remaining motionless above the
Swiss Alps while the Earth continued spinning below.

In the U.S., artists began their own projects, inspired by the
newly possible private-access to space: Frank Pietronigro has
explored queer theory relative to creating diversity among future
space travelers already in the late 90's and Trevor Paglen has
recently launched a project on the EchoStar XVI communications
satellite that may stay in orbit for millions of years.

Carrie Paterson has developed perfumes for *Homesickness
Kits* for future space farers; and Bradley Pitts has created an
immersive video installation in which he attempts to capture the
missed and often subtle experiences during a low-gravity,
parabolic training flight. And now there are private companies,
such as *XCOR Aerospace*, which will initiate sub-orbital flights, and
Final Frontier Design—one of whose founding members comes out
of costume design—that is developing garments for space travel.

Additionally, in this same time period several artists
looked at the new developments from the viewpoint of a cultural
anthropologist, such as *Center for Land Use Interpretation's*
documentation of experimental plane sites at Edwards Air Force
Base, which is adjacent to the Mojave Space and Air Port and
Connie Samaras' large-scale photographs of Spaceport America
under construction in New Mexico. One of the commissioned
projects for *Free Enterprise* is by eteam. They traveled to the towns
of Moon and Mars, both in Pennsylvania, and created a video work

about how each town has embraced its celestial namesake.

Artists are now creating their own institutional frameworks for cooperative interaction with the wider space and culture communities. Two such projects and initiatives are represented in *Free Enterprise*. The Slovenian *KSEVT (Cultural Center of European Space Technologies)* from Vitanje, a unique transdisciplinary initiative and a remarkable architectural structure, brings culture and the arts to the forefront of space exploration paradigms. *ETTAS (European Space Agency Topical Team Arts and Science)*, provides a pragmatic approach for artists and scientists connected to the *European Space Agency Human Spaceflight* division to open up the ESA structures to artistic and cultural collaboration, intervention and creation. And artists have begun to chronicle the new developments in private space enterprise in creative and aesthetically inventive documents. The showcased book, *Chase for Space*, by Nejc Trošt is one recent example. Additionally, Skeith De Wine has created the *California Leonardo da Vinci Discovery* in an effort to create a modern day place where science, engineering, and the arts can coexist, just as they did in Leonardo's mind and speculative inventions, many of which included methods for human flight.

These initiatives by private citizens rather than state agencies that aim to fuse the science of space exploration with the speculations of artists is one reason that *Free Enterprise* does includes an early twentieth-century constructivist conceptual work (coincidentally one elaborated by an international collective of artists in Trieste in 1927) that paved the way in the understanding of the meaning of non-gravitational spaces in the context of art; the unique conceptualization of the KSEVT Cultural Centre of European Space Technologies, the first institution devoted primarily to the connections between the arts and sciences of space in the world; and the fantastic and visionary work of XCOR engineers in the same context. In essence, they all belong together as part of the same visionary paradigm.

The goal of this conceptual collaborative matrix between the industry and artists is to match the enthusiasm, sense of adventure, and creative process that is shared by both the space exploration entrepreneurs and visionaries and the artists who have explored the subject for many years. Both take the risk to expend personal intellectual, immaterial and material capital, never knowing quite what the return will be on their dreams to expand the reach of humanity beyond Earth—a dream, which has to be noted, historically started in the arts, philosophy and literature, and not in the basic or applied sciences and technology. From earliest times our sense of self has been defined by our sense of presence in the universe. The heavens have been our most significant metaphor for inspiration and vastness, voyage and possibility. *Free Enterprise: The Art of Citizen Space Exploration* demonstrates how artists, engineers and scientists are not only redefining that metaphor, but also moving beyond metaphor by achieving innovative cultural and artistic expression. □

Manifest Destination in *Spaceport America* by Connie Samaras

(2012)

Connie Samaras' large-scale photographs document a reality that seems unreal. Her subjects are not what we see in the photographs, but the ambivalent forces behind them: human ingenuity, global capitalism, and imaginations of the future. Their scale and luscious colors of the photographs suggest a celebration of the built environment in some of the most impossible places to reach—arctic, desert, and outer space—but also as warnings as to where these endeavors may lead, ambiguities embodied in Samaras' 2010-11 series, *Spaceport America*.

Built in in a remote location between Truth or Consequences and Las Cruces, New Mexico, the architecture is reminiscent of the terminal designed by Eero Saarinen for the Trans World Flight Center, which opened in 1962 at JFK Airport. Charged with capturing "the spirit of flight," Saarinen created a design to suggest a bird's wings in flight. One of the unique aspects to its design was soaring windows to allow passengers to view departing and arriving flights, that is, to witness human imagination, initiative, and inventiveness.

For Spaceport America, the architectural firm, Foster+Partners write on their website with words evocative of sentiments about the TWA terminal: "The sinuous shape of the building in the landscape and its interior spaces seek to capture the drama and mystery of space flight itself, articulating the thrill of space travel for the first space tourists." It is hard not to see similarities between the two terminals that include both soaring wings and windows.

In Samaras' photographs, she captures the in-progress building of Spaceport America. The desert landscape is depicted as barren. People are absent, as if the architecture rose from the ground, its material nature ready to launch our ephemeral desires to leave Earth. *Terminal Construction, Entrance, 2010*, shot at a distance, depicts the terminal merged with the horizon, and finally *Terminal Hanging Facility, Facing Mission Control, 2010* is from the runway view and the terminal looks like a stereotypical, saucer-shaped UFO that has just landed, as if intentionally alluding to a pop culture imaginary.

At first glance, Samaras' compositional approach, found in much of her work from the past decade, is an impassive one that creates a liminal space for the viewer, who is then forced to negotiate Samaras' seemingly ambiguous stance: is she simply documenting a building or trying to examine the fraught spirit of progress that the building unknowingly expresses?

But, with other project titles in this survey exhibition like *Surface Events* (2007) and *After the American Century* (2009), Samaras' sentiments clearly lean toward questioning a future imaginary that embodies a utopian desire for creating the perfect society through technological means: will the high-tech provide enhance the human condition or will it progressively remove independence? Or, are these the wrong questions.

Spaceport America's setting captures represents these clashing attitudes. It is in the desert, which has often been a site to seek salvation, as it is a place of distance from civilization and its distractions. The hardship of its harsh environment is also a test for one's spiritual will. But this notion subtly casts the desert as blank slate, a characterization that endures today. In other words, it is a geography considered absent of *human* history, and therefore, has no history. Yet, this desert and any land do have a history. Consider the Apaches who may have bathed in nearby hot springs, who ground seeds into flour in rock mortars, or determined geographical sites as a sacred, perhaps consider as places of mythical and spiritual birth.

Samaras considers the use of the desert as a backdrop for imaging the future in her *After the American Century* series too. It focuses on the rampant construction in the Arabian city of Dubai and employs one of the major, invisible arms of global capitalism: harsh labor conditions in a harsh environment.

In this light, Samaras' return to New Mexico, where she was raised in her early years, is a return not to her past but to the future in documenting a very real built environment but one that speculates on the future of humankind. Its location in a state that was the site for Cold War nuclear bomb development, for continued secret military bases, and for a tourism that visits the intersection of Western and indigenous cultures, Spaceport America unknowingly embodies today's global capitalism that takes the basic attitude of "Just Build It, Just Do It" and let the consequences drive future policy. However, Samaras' oeuvre suggests that the all these futurisms could really be giving birth to another Manifest Destiny. □

Miguel Palma: An Artistic Exploration of the Sonoran Desert by a Human Alien

(2013)

Miguel Palma was born on Earth in Lisbon, Portugal. This is a fact. However, one of his most recent, multifaceted projects at Arizona State University Art Museum, *Trajectory*, commissioned in 2011-12 for the *Desert Initiative: Desert One* project, indicated his desire to look toward the stars. He was also fascinated with the idea of going to outer space in order to see Earth from afar, as if an alien, though still retaining his human identification. The heart of Palma's project was a repurposed 1985 M1008 CUCV troop carrier. It was outfitted with video cameras in order to document and gather data as Palma traveled the Sonoran desert for nearly ten months during his residency.

The impetus to "explore" the desert, as if it were the same arid region found on the Moon or Mars, and to do so with an invention of his own making, harkens back to his childhood. In his early teens, during the 1970s, he built model rockets, sending up plastic soldier payloads that would return to Earth by parachute, and he also spent hours looking at the stars through his backyard telescope in Lisbon. When not attempting to escape Earth's gravity with his own miniature rocket, he would work on other model kits, but he would more than likely not follow the enclosed instructions purposefully. In other words, Palma's childhood delights of gazing at the stars and of creating new challenges for oneself by ignoring the rules have formed threads that run throughout his peripatetic, international art career.

The *Desert Initiative: Desert One* project is based on the notion of reinvisioning Earth in terms of its twenty-two deserts, as opposed to the oceans or rainforests. In this respect, artists from other arid regions are invited to ASU or are brought there to explore the surrounding Sonoran desert. The desert is fraught with symbolism that ranges from spiritual journeys to secret military bases. Many people consider the desert a vast land of lifeless sand before they have a chance to visit it, which was Palma's own viewpoint before his arrival.

In light of recent wars initiated by the U.S. in the desert lands of the Middle East, such as Iraq and Afghanistan, it seems most appropriate that Palma initiated his journey into an American desert with a military vehicle that was reframed as a roving sculpture and data collection device. Ultimately, he ended up commiserating with astronauts completing geology training at SP Crater North outside of Flagstaff, Arizona. (The landscape is a terrain indicative of the lunar surface, so that the astronauts can practice moving in space suits and driving a lunar rover.) In this respect, there is a merging of Earth and its arid planet neighbors within this extreme environment of the desert.

In preparation for the intense temperatures and in imitation of climate controlled astronaut suits, Palma built his own wearable cooling system. He attached sixty fans to an astronaut-orange jumpsuit. It not only served a practical purpose but also helped to frame his viewpoint as a "stranger in a strange land." His self-proclaimed mission was to have no mission. Or, perhaps, the only mission was to leave the desert oasis of Phoenix and venture out into the arid lands that so many of the city's residents did not seem to embrace, at least that was Palma's sense of the community's relationship to its environment.

While on his human/alien road trip, he made 100 drawings about Arizona. This number was meant to correspond to Arizona's centennial in 2012. They were inspired by popular magazines from the 1940s to the 60s, such as *Arizona Highways*, that romanticized the state, despite its extreme environment. His drawings incorporated collaged elements, like a camping trailer, with Palma's own graphic riffs on how these past representations gelled with today's reality. They were hung in the exhibition by binder clips on stretched metal wire; an exhibition design that captured the fleeting and various thoughts that Palma had on his journey. The hanging also suggested an old-fashioned laundry line. However, instead of clothes being set out to dry in the sun, they were old ideas about Arizona and the desert that needed cleansing.

Palma also made a set of thirty-one monoprints, titled *Up and Down* collectively, that explored Felix Baumgartner's recent, groundbreaking and record setting stunt in 2012, *Red Bull Stratos*. He jumped to Earth from a helium balloon in the stratosphere in October 2012; setting the altitude record for a manned balloon flight at 39 kilometers (24 miles), parachute jump from the highest altitude, and greatest free fall velocity, breaking the sound barrier at Mach 1.25.

Palma was most interested in what he viewed as a kind of reversal of space exploration by Baumgartner. Instead of aiming for another celestial body, such as the Moon or Mars, his aim was to head towards space, although not in outer space, in order to see Earth from a distance, and then descend, as if a human who had become an extraterrestrial, at least that was the metaphor that Palma saw in this daredevil's exploit. It is the same viewpoint that Palma took towards his trek into the desert. This notion was perhaps captured best by Robert Heinlein's 1961 speculative fiction novel, *Stranger in a Strange Land.* It tells the story of Valentine Michael Smith, a human who comes to Earth in early adulthood after being born on the planet Mars and raised by Martians. In essence, the novel explores the definition of what it means to be human, and the subsequent rights and privileges that come with the status. The same ethical, thought experiment in fiction has been illustrated with human-like machines that develop their own intelligence and emotions, yet are treated as less-than human, like slaves in human history.

In today's space tourism literature distributed by companies like Virgin Galactic or XCOR Aerospace, who are on the verge of successful private enterprise launches into suborbital space, a huge policy shift in the U.S. government away from state sponsored missions by NASA, one finds an emphasis on witnessing the curvature of Earth as part of the experience. In other words, they sense that people want to experience the indelible 1969 image of seeing Earth from the Moon, of being reminded of our small place in the universe in order to be prompted to think cosmically and, perhaps, to have a little bit of that alien feeling of approaching a "new planet" for the first time.

This emphasis on one's viewpoint was underscored by the first experience in Palma's exhibition at ASU. It was a video projection of a mysterious set of objects, such as toy figures, books, and crumbling buildings, and what would seem the detritus of American pop culture. It was not until the end of the exhibition on the third floor that its source was discovered.

An eight-foot diameter platform turned very slowly and was powered by a hacked power drill. The piece was called *In Image We Trust.* There was a model of an F16 fighter jet jutting above the conglomeration of toys and domestic items with a small surveillance camera in its nose. The large kinetic sculpture did not play music, although it mimicked a record player, but played a live feed back to the museum entrance. Viewers were left to reconcile the two experiences of seeing the world through lenses and technology versus seeing the real objects. It was akin to how we perceive the universe—through telescopes and sensors—and also how we view our perceived enemies in faraway deserts through cameras mounted to bombs and drones. Again, Palma was being sensitive to the effects of technology on how we view the world.

In another piece, *Erosion,* which was inspired by the geology of the planets, Palma placed volcanic stones from SP Crater, north of Flagstaff, into a thick, plastic cylinder. It was spun by another hacked power drill. At the beginning, the plastic was clear, shining, and beautiful, and the rocks were hard and intact. But, over time, the plastic became polished and whiter from scratch marks.

The stones pummeled one another into dust. This work was about the fragility of even the seemingly most powerful substances, such as stones. It was also about entropy; things changing into another state, never able to return to its original state. Entropy was a concept that American earthwork artist Robert Smithson explored endlessly in the 1960s and 70s. Several projects were mounted in desert environments, such as the *Spiral Jetty* in Utah from 1970.

There were many other works in the show, such as *Action Plan,* that displayed GI Joe and Action Man toy action figures, along with their toy guns and boats, like a specimen display in a natural history museum; and *Spectrum (Images from Raven, a Robotic Assisted Vehicle for Extraterrestrial Exploration),* which involved projecting slides of the Arizona landscape that appeared alien, as they images were taken through one of twelve filters on a special Mini-Thermal Emission Spectrometer (Mini-TES) camera, a replica of those on-board the Mars rovers in order to detect different minerals in the rocks. Conceptually, all of the works in the show formed a "trajectory," as the title suggested, but it was a circuitous one. It was not a straight shot into orbit or to the Moon, but for Palma it was one meant to harken back to his indelible childhood memories of wanting to go into outer space; to explore an exotic and harsh landscape; to explore how a state sees itself after 100 years; to consider how technology shapes our viewpoint of the world; and how to act as a citizen scientist exploring new possibilities as access to space travel increases. He was able to wrestle with all of these ideas at once in *Trajectory* by shifting his viewpoint from that of an indigenous Earthling. Rather, he saw himself as a human visiting the planet from a different point of view—one that came from his imagination rather than through a lens. □

A Reconsideration of Fourth of July Fireworks and Independence Day in Light of Cai Guo-Qiang's *Sky Ladder*
(2012)

The United States of America adopted the Declaration of Independence on July 4, 1776, in which the nascent thirteen colonies professed its freedom from the control of the British Empire. The day is known as either Independence Day or the Fourth of July. Its most iconic celebrations are with a parade during the day and fireworks in the evening. In Riverside, California, a grand display of pyrotechnics is shot from the top of Mount Rubidoux each year.

The Chinese invented gunpowder in 7th century B.C., which led to all sorts of explosive devices, such as fireworks, which eventually led up to the technology that allowed humans to escape the earth's gravity into outer space atop skyscraper-sized bottle rockets. The U.S. owes not only debt to this ancient Chinese technology but, today, is in major financial debt to China. We're not as independent as we'd like to think, despite celebrating Independence Day.

On this day of sending projectiles above the city that burst into patterns called Chrysanthemum, Ring, Spider, and Salute, among others, the irony of economic dependence to a country whose technology allowed the U.S to excel in the aerospace industry seem embodied to me in the work of a Chinese-born, New

York-based artist Cai Guo-Qiang, whose work happens to be on display in Los Angeles. He is known for creating public spectacles with fireworks and using them to create more traditional drawings for hanging, but with a very non-traditional technique based on pyrotechnics. His exhibition, *Sky Ladder*, at The Museum of Contemporary Art in Los Angeles, is on view through July 30, 2012, and is the first West Coast solo museum exhibition work by Cai.

For Cai, his work is not an attempt to compete with Fourth of July of celebrations or Disney's nightly firework displays, about an hour's drive from downtown L.A. to Anaheim in Orange County. His spectacles are aimed less at being entertaining with their abstract beauty of lights in the sky, and more as an exploration into using them to communicate with other intelligent beings in outer space, letting them know that "We're here!"

By directing our attention skyward with the hope of life beyond earth, then perhaps we'll forget seeming differences between humans that lead to war, colonization, and economic indebtedness. In other words, hopefully there will be no more need for wars of independence.

Cai embodies these sentiments in his titles, such as *Mystery Circle: Explosion Project for MOCA, Los Angeles.* It is the latest work in Cai's *Projects for Extraterrestrials* series that began in 1989 and has since included more than thirty works. Located on the northern exterior wall of The Geffen Contemporary at MOCA, the piece was ignited on April 7, 2012, to create a spectacular explosion, including pyrotechnic flying saucers, burning crop circles, and an alien god.

One way in which Cai attempts some galactic transnationalism is to enlist members of the community where each project takes place to assist in the set up, managing the event, and so on. Just as he changes physically the gunpowder into ephemeral images on the side of a building or on paper, he also attempts to change cultural habits through a community effort with mutual purpose that is, simply put, about "communication." Perhaps in the back of Cai's mind, he hopes that there may be an "alien" in the crowd too who gets his message?

However, the results of said communication could result in disaster, as represented in the 1996 movie, *Independence Day*. It is an apocalyptic, science fiction film in which aliens invade Earth on July 2nd. Humans attack back with their biggest affront being on the Fourth of July! Director and screenwriter of the film, Roland Emmerich, demonstrates that a common threat can unite people, unlike Cai who focuses on communication rather than annihilation as the hoped for interaction.

In 1950s sci-fi films, alien invasions could also be viewed as stand-ins for the Communist threat in the American cultural imagination, e.g. Red Mars/Red Communism. Will the Chinese become the new malevolent Martians? Cai's community-based actions, spectacles, and unique use of homegrown gunpowder technology would suggest otherwise. But, will American mainstream cinema follow suit, or will it create more stories to instill fear? After all, the Chinese have been sending their citizens to space and are even building their own space lab. Will they be the first to colonize the Moon or Mars, creating a Peoples Republic of

Luna? But these types of nationalistic anxieties are exactly what Cai wants to avoid in his own work by aiming towards more universal goals of communication by any means possible, even via explosives.

On this Fourth of July, while I sit on another tall hillside, able to see not only the fireworks from Mount Rubidoux but also from many of the surrounding Inland Empire cities—giving the appearance of a shock-and-awe, under-the-of-night bombardment of the region—I ask myself, "What is independence?"

In a twisted kind of logic in which the U.S. pays homage to its new masters, can the use of fireworks for a Fourth of July in 2012 be viewed as a reluctant celebration of economic dependence on China, eschewing 236 years of independence from the British Empire? I exaggerate, of course. Because, the truth, is that we humans are dependent deep down, but on one another, not on nation states or a global economy—at least, that's how it should be. I believe that Cai is after the same ideal. He goes further by inspiring ties between humans and other intelligent creatures. In this view, Independence Day is a misnomer for we are (in) Dependence in reality.

Slaves, the colonized, and those in servitude have known that independence lies in one's mind. So, even if your body is broken, your mind is alive, able to protect one's true self. It is the one place that cannot yet be actively reached by others—although influences from the outside are possible of course—but no permanent sensors, probes, and chips as of yet. So, for me, my fireworks are not explosions in the sky, but the electrical ones by neurons in my brain. □

Presence Machines: Philip K. Dick's Roman Empire and *The Imaginary 20th Century*

(2008)

A suspicion that the Roman Empire is still under construction arises in me while visiting Orange County's largest shopping mall, South Coast Plaza.

I stop at Orange County Museum of Art's satellite gallery, the Orange Lounge, in the Plaza to experience *The Imaginary 20th Century*. It is an interactive science-fiction novel that includes a database of more than 2,000 images amassed from various archives. The story focuses on the adventures of a woman, who, in the year 1901, selects four suitors to seduce her, each with their own vision for the new century.

Inside a black box gallery, at the rear of the Lounge, I stand at a pedestal and use a white mouse to navigate the database of images that are projected mural-size on the opposite wall, while a disembodied voice reads the text aloud from a selected chapter. The main character, a progressive thinking woman, touches on many social issues, such as the suffrage of women. They would not be given the vote nationally in the U.S. until 1920, nineteen years into her future.

The architectonics in the future makes an impression on me too. Their aesthetic consists mainly of a plethora of steel frames. This was a technique that would allow buildings to surpass the limits of load-bearing masonry, and become skyscrapers, as we would come to know them after 1901. The limitations of an imagined future are portrayed in these late 19th-century images, as they are based on the knowledge of what was then present. My interpretation of *The Imaginary 20th Century*'s engineering images, along with the experience of viewing in it in a mall within OC, resurrects in my mind the writings of famed sci-fi author Philip K. Dick. He moved to OC in 1972, settling in Fullerton at first. What manner of architecture surrounded PKD in OC at his last residence in Santa Ana when he died in 1982 from a heart attack?

I leave South Coast Plaza and drive a few miles north to what I believe to be his old condo building on Civic Center Drive. The building is what I would describe as quintessential Le-California-Corbusier: stucco exterior, stacked floors, and a density of units.

The building's oblong stockiness reminds me of an experience that I had in Fresno two weeks earlier on 2-25-08. One evening, I drove around the city and ended up at River Park Shopping Center. It was replete with Borders, Starbucks, Anne Taylor Loft, and most of the box stores that form shopping islands throughout the western desert. I was struck suddenly with an uncanny feeling while I navigated the open-air walkways. Had I ever left OC?

The familiarity of the stores, and their specific organization into an old-fashion, city-block, shopping experience, like The Grove in Los Angeles or Victoria Gardens in Rancho

Cucamonga, disconnected me from Fresno. For a few moments, I could not recall that I had drove four hours north. I was in Fresno and OC simultaneously. But it was not in the sense of a double-body, like one of Dick's stories, where the human and his android look-alike live separately. Rather, it was more like recognizing stasis, as if I had been born indeed, but had never moved out of my New Orleans hospital crib.

A current resident of Dick's old stucco condo building exits, walks across the street, and enters Saint Joseph Church. The security gate is left ajar. I walk into the inner cement courtyard. It is dreary and lackluster. I can only guess which condo was PKD's.

I stand here for a bit trying to imagine what Dick would refer to as his 2-3-74 experience; twenty-four years later from my own 2-25-08 experience in Fresno. Dick's story, as he has wrote about it, said that a girl delivering pain medication from a dentist was wearing a gold *ichthys*, the Christian emblem of two intersecting arcs that form the profile of a fish. Dick claimed that the symbol's impact on his mind, perhaps enhanced by his constantly drug infused constitution, was *anamnesis*, that is, the lifting of amnesia, allowing him to see the world as it was really.

Subsequent to this revelation, he believed that the progress of history stopped in the 1st century A.D., and that the Roman Empire never ended. For him, the Empire represented the extreme of a materialistic and unspiritual world point of view. The result was that the world's population was enslaved by its possessions, along with other assorted emotional ailments.

Dick's cosmogny shared kinship with Gnosticism; a belief system which teaches that humans are souls trapped in a material world created by an defective spirit. However, the soul may be returned to the divine realm through a process of awakening. Additionally, God would come to know itself fully again only after all humans achieved salvation, meaning a release from their worldly paraphernalia, thus, the end of the Roman Empire.

My experience at South Coast Plaza of perusing the images presented in *The Imaginary 20th Century* served to remind me that no matter how hard people may try, their ideas of the future will tend to be situated in the present. Additionally, they may do so in a manner complicit with the Roman Empire's prophetic and psychic reach through the centuries, when they opt for the architectural bliss and false security of hyperreal, stucco, shopping islands. Also, I realize that when I was in Fresno, I grasped for a moment that the ancient, load-bearing masonry of an empire stretching from Italy to Britain and Germany to North Africa and the Persian Gulf is still being built. □

Part V

Desert Mythos

Levitating the Archaic Mind with Michael Heizer's *Levitated Mass*

(2012)

During the Neolithic Age, there were human societies who erected megalithic structures to mark the summer solstice, the longest day of the year. When the sun rose, its rays streaming through post-and-lintel structures, as at Stonehenge (constructed between 3100 to 2000 BC), in just the perfect calculated arrangement, it was a time when the Earth and the Sky met, when the gravity of earth pulled downwards the life of the sun, celebrating fertility. In this sacred geography, the physical and spiritual worlds met and departed. Today, the Western mind may view the ritual as fascinating but quaint, as there's no business plan attached to it.

Michael Heizer's *Levitated Mass*, a permanent installation scheduled to open to the public on the campus of the Los Angeles County Museum of Art on Sunday, June 24, 2012, is just four days after this year's solstice on June 20th.

In light of this date, the process behind the creation of the work, and even its proximity to the La Brea Tar Pits from which thousands of millennia old bones have been excavated, it is hard not to envision the project as a contemporary revival of creating something sacred, though secular, within the confines of a world where everything seems to have its price.

There are many parallels between the archaic and the contemporary, which can be seen, by example, in what we have surmised from studying the development of Stonehenge. It is has been estimated by archaeologists, such as Mike Parker Pearson, leader of the Stonehenge Riverside Project, that it took nearly 1,500 years to construct Stonehenge through its various stages.

For Stonehenge, sarsen granite blocks, one of the densest and hardest of stones, were transported from southwest Wales, some two hundred miles away. One theory about the distant source of materials, developed by a research team associated with the Royal College of Art in London, is that this particular granite sounded like bells when struck by another stone. In essence, spirits would seem to be living in the rocks and speaking. Thus, these particular stones had-to-be-had.

Similarly, in what now seems a legend in the making, as the story has become repeated often in newspaper articles, Heizer conceived of his project in 1968, and has been looking for the perfect boulder since that time. Then one day in 2006, someone from the prior owner of the quarry, Paul J. Hubbs Construction, contacted Heizer, as he was someone with whom Heizer had worked in the past, and said that the "perfect rock" was there. It had been blasted off a hillside at what is now Stone Valley Materials. But it was too big and solid for the quarry to use it for their purposes of producing concrete aggregate and sand. So it sat there, nearly two-stories tall at 21 feet in height and weighing 340 tons.

Once Heizer was alerted of the rock's existence and after checking it out at the quarry when he was there to select big rocks for other projects, and seeing its resemblance to the rock in his early sketches from 1968, he contacted Michael Govan, LACMA's director. Govan has been quoted in the Los Angeles Times as saying, "Mike was calling from the Ontario airport and said: 'I found this amazing rock,'" Govan said. "He referred to it as the Colossi of Memnon and compared it to the great pink granite Egyptian obelisks for the quality of the stone. He said it was one of the greatest rocks he'd ever seen."

The legend of its find seems to increase with each article because Govan has become the de facto spokesman for Heizer on this work, in light of the artist's reluctance to engage with the media. In other words, without Heizer's direct answers, then interpretation and guesswork will abound, thus, adding to "the mystery of the rock."

In the time of Stonehenge, hundreds of people would be required to transport just one stone, taking weeks, months, and perhaps years. Trees would be felled on site in order to create a rolling track—this was a time just before the use of the wheel as a widespread method of transport.

For Heizer's rock, the Oregon-based company, Emmert was hired to transport the rock from the Jurupa Valley, just west of the city of Riverside, for its 105-mile journey to the LACMA campus. It went from a dusty, lowly populated valley in the Colorado desert to the Mid-Wilshire district in Los Angeles, a strip once called the Miracle Mile for its quick rise to commercial prominence in the first half of the twentieth-century. Just as the sarsen stone would have been transported through a variety of rival, tribal territories, the rock was carried across four counties: San Bernardino, Riverside, Orange, and Los Angeles, and twenty-two cities. However, there were no reported incidents of tribal warring. No arrows were shot, stones thrown, or even bartering for passage, other than with city permits.

Akin to felling the trees for transport in the ancient past, a rolling technology for Heizer's boulder had to be developed on site. Emmert is a company that moves "what other people don't want to or can't handle...like nuclear power plants," according to Emmert engineer Rick Albrecht in a video produced by LACMA that documents the rocks transport. The solution by the company was to bring huge, steel trusses that sat on either side of the rock and then steel cables were wrapped under and cradled it during transport. In the end, the transporter was 200-feet long, had 176 wheels, and moved at a top speed of 8 mph through southern California.

As in the ancient past, and during such a long journey for hauling the sarsen block, I'm sure that there were moments of celebration, especially when an especially hard obstacle was overcome. Similarly, at one stop in Long Beach's Bixby Knolls neighborhood, a block party was held with thousands of people in attendance. On videos, you can see people coming up to touch the rock. The fact that it was shrunk wrapped in white plastic to protect the rock added an air of mystery to it. What could be so special about this rock after all?

After eleven days of travel in March, the rock arrived at the LACMA campus, where it was installed on a 456-foot-long concrete slot near the museum's Resnick Pavilion. Once on site, the museum's context as a showcase for art from around the world and different time periods, along with Heizer's artistic intent, transformed an unusable rock at a Riverside quarry into the sculpture, "Levitated Mass."

Four days after this year's summer solstice on June 20, 2012, people will gather at "Levitated Mass" on June 24. Visitors will be able to walk down from either end of the slot, slowly descending to a center point, fifteen feet under the boulder, where it will have the feeling of being lighter than air, hence, *Levitated Mass*.

As visitors walk under it, they may contemplate the geomorphology of Earth as shaped by land (tectonic plates), wind (Aeolian), water (fluvial), and fire (volcanism). Others may consider the work in an art historical context, thinking it radical that they can view its base, as this side of sculpture is usually relegated to facing a floor or a pedestal. Perhaps there will be some new actions by The Aetherius Society, based just a few miles north in Hollywood. This is a spiritual group that was founded in 1955 and one of their main tenets is to charge selected Holy Mountains with prayer, like spiritual batteries, in order to uplift and heal the world. Maybe they will want to pray around "Levitated Mass" and charge the boulder?

Reflecting on a lineage with sacred sites of the ancient past, LACMA's director, Michael Govan, says, while visiting the rock in the quarry before its transport, "There's a very ancient tradition in ancient cultures ranging from Egyptian cultures to the Olmec in

Mexico of moving monoliths to mark a place. And I think the idea is that LACMA's campus is a multicultural center of Los Angeles and this rock will mark this in a weighty and timeless manner."

Interestingly, Heizer's sculpture sits on the opposite side of Chris Burden's *Urban Light* sculpture on Wilshire. His work is a gridded placement of old street lamps with varying heights, as if to suggest the congestion of an urban environment but also the excitement of not knowing what's around the corner of a building, along with evoking the magic that city lights can produce at night. Then in LACMA's "backyard" there will be Heizer's *Levitated Mass* now. There, it feels like a sculpture that one might find in the desert: an arid landscape allowing distant viewing of monumental, geographic features.

It shares kinship with his other site-specific, land art sculptures such as his 1969 work "Double Negative," in which he moved tons of rock to create ramps at Mormon Mesa in a remote area of southeast Nevada, and is now owned by The Museum of Contemporary Art, Los Angeles (MOCA). Ironically, neither this work nor the artist are included, at Heizer's request, in MOCA's current exhibition, *Ends of the Earth: Land Art to 1974*, on view through September 3rd.

Earthworks or Land art were works created in nature, merging with the landscape, rather than plopped upon it. Many of the works were created in the deserts of Nevada, New Mexico, Utah and Arizona. Rising out of conceptual and minimalist art, it was in part a reaction against the commercialization and decontextualized

containment within the walls of galleries and museums. Perhaps
Heizer still adheres to this principle?

Coincidentally, thirty years ago, another artist, Lewis
deSoto, now based in northern California, but who was born and
raised in Riverside did a project that looked at the history of
another granite hill, not far from Jurupa Valley, that was turned
into the materials for cement.

deSoto's fascination with transformation of sacred
landscapes can be found in a seminal, early, photo-based project,
created just out of graduate school, and exhibited at UCR's
California Museum of Photography, *The Tahualtapa Project*, 1983-
1988. Its name refers to "The Hill of the Ravens" in Cahuilla lore.
The mountain in the San Bernardino Valley was later known as Mt.
Slover, and for nearly twelve decades, the presence of the
California Portland Cement plant in Colton, not far from Riverside,
mined limestone and used 3,000-degree kilns to turn it into clinker
bricks, and then ground the clinker into cement powder. It was the
first such producer of cement in the United States. For this project,
deSoto employed in his photographs a running motif that
represented the outline of the once existing mountain. In essence,
the project explored the theme of how a sacred mountain was
transformed by both renaming it and grinding it down into the
materials for the cities of a different kind of civilization.

However, this is not to say that although Tahualtapa has
been transformed into cement, there is still spiritual power in its
transformed state as cement material. Objects are not dead but
alive, and should therefore be approached not only with curiosity,

but respect. Or as Lewis deSoto said in a January 2012 lecture on his work at UCR Culver Center of the Arts, "Everyday objects have energy too. They can be power objects that carry an idea forward. Nothing is anonymous and everything is authored."

deSoto's use of the word "authored" does remind me that the "earthworks" movement, with which Heizer is affiliated, was a phrase appropriated from the title of a 1965 novel, *Earthworks*, by Brian Aldiss, a British science fiction author.

This origin tale for the movement's moniker having come from the science fiction genre makes it unavoidable for me to consider how the future will look back at *Levitated Mass*. Today will be the future's past in the end. What will they ask when they look back, like we do with Stonehenge, attempting to interpret its ring of megaliths? What is the rock's purpose? How was it moved? Was it part of a religion? Why did the people feel the need to move it here from a distant quarry? Why couldn't the quarry have been made the sacred site instead?

"Earthworks" is a dystopian story set in a world of environmental catastrophe and extreme socio-economic inequality. In 1967, the artist Robert Smithson took a copy of it with him on a trip to the Passaic River in New Jersey, out of which he published the highly influential piece in 1967, "A Tour of the Monuments of Passaic," a meditation on time and place, the definition of what is sculpture, and on entropy, especially as it relates to the environment: once something is changed, it cannot go back to what it was before.

Under Smithson's influence, *Earthworks* became the title of the first group exhibition to gather like-minded artists that was held at the Virginia Dwan Gallery in New York from October 5th to the 30th in 1968. The artists who were included were Carl Andre, Walter De Maria, Robert Smithson, and Michael Heizer, among many others.

So, in homage to Aldiss, Smithson, Dwan, and Heizer, here is one fanciful speculation on how future humans will interpret *Levitated Mass*, attempting to connect their interpretation to the ancient human cultures of 2012:

It does not represent a desire to conquest nature, but rather, in one of the last efforts known at transporting and making a megalith, it represented a desire to reconnect with the sacred, which is the planet itself. However, humans had already pitched the planet beyond the return point of sustaining their lives, as they knew them. But this rock has endured. And human intelligence endured, albeit not in a humanoid form. Rather, we Galactics now live in this and other rocks. We commune with magma down to the planet's core and sense the happenings on the planet's surface. We are unmoving, but ready to sing and talk when another mobile being beats another rock against one of our sides. Then we will talk and sing the story of humankind's primal desire to move elements of the land. How this will be interpreted and acted upon will be the story of these beings, whomever they may be. □

The Idyll-Beast: A Wild Child Imaginary in Idyllwild, California

(2012)

Our species' past or future is about an hour's drive, due east from Riverside, in the mountain hamlet of Idyllwild. There, the Idyll-Beast is said to exist—a creature akin to Bigfoot, or Sasquatch. This Inland Empire creature has been described as being between seven and fifteen feet in height, weighing between 300 and 1,000 pounds, is usually seen as erect, walking with a swinging ape-like gait, and is covered in shaggy hair or fur. This description is similar to those of other Bigfoots throughout the country. However, in a brochure from a research center dedicated to studying the creature, "Idyllbeast: Myth or Monster?," purportedly issued by the San Bernardino National Forest San Jacinto Ranger District for the "Safe and Sane Behavior Around Native Non-Human Hominids," there are details described that are perhaps unique to the Idyll-Beast: "No one who looks an Idyllbeast [sic] in the face will soon forget its intense glowing eyes and sardonic smirk. On winter nights the call of the Idyllbeast echoes eerily through the quiet air, causing animals to whimper and humans to lock their doors and consult their [real estate] brokers. Sometimes the creatures are reported to have a curious garlicky odor."

The Idyll-Beast is a fabrication, as you may have guessed. The creature's originator is David Jerome, an Idyllwild musician and guitar instructor. He is also the director of the Idyll-Beast

Research Center Museum and Gift Shoppe, which is housed in a side area of Steve Moulton's Bubba Books. Jerome's statements about the creature in print and on TV are elusive, though he retains a prankster's smirk. Whatever the original motivation, the Idyll-Beast has been embraced by the townspeople as a source of pride and tourist income. In an effort to protect the beast and the community's consensual hallucination, the aforementioned brochure states, "the Idyll-Beast is protected under the California Rare, Endangered and Imaginary Creature Act of 2005."

Just before entering Idyllwild, there is sometimes found, as they are often stolen, a yellow diamond yield sign with a silhouette of the beast made out of fur and can be found posted along Highway 243. The beast, that is, a man in a Wookie-like costume, even appears at public functions, most importantly during the Fourth of July weekend parade, which includes an Idyll-Beast Festival. He also helps market the mountain community by attending events such as the Riverside County Fair and National Date Festival in Indio.

However, I'm less attracted to Jerome's and the town of Idyllwild's expressions of quirky, artistic, prankster sensibilities, and more interested in the seeming desire for the creature to exist. I'm interested with how this desire connects with a larger cultural expression that wants to believe that a wild side of humankind still exists, even if out there and not in us.

For me, the Idyll-Beast represents speculation on the ascent of man, a need to control the environment, and a comment upon human self-delusion about ignoring our loss of contact with nature. I think that the motivation for purporting the creature's existence comes from a larger desire to believe that there is a primitive side of us that is still alive and walking with an ape-like gait. I don't believe that the creature will ever be caught, whether in the Pacific Northwest or SoCal's Inland Empire, because it will mean that the last vestige of humankind's wildness will have been tamed and, thus, eradicated.

Perhaps, we all want to believe that there exists a "wild child," like Victor of Aveyron found in France in 1797 during Napoleonic times in south of France. He lived as a feral child, surviving without language or human agency. His feral state was fascinating, as evidenced by the numerous dramatizations and documentaries on Victor, such as François Truffaut's *L'Enfant sauvage* (1970). In fact, during Victor's time, Enlightenment ideas decentered the place of humans as special, viewing them as part of nature, rather than separate, whereby they could justify reigning supreme over the other animals and plants; a sentiment supported by the Bible, Genesis 1:26 (King James version), "And God said, Let us make man in our image, after our likeness: and let them have dominion over the fish of the sea, and over the fowl of the air, and over the cattle, and over all the earth, and over every creeping thing that creepeth upon the earth." It was thought then that studying Victor might detect the signs of that transition from proto-human to modern human.

But, over 200 years later, we are still very mannered. The impulse is to wear a nice jacket rather than a letting our body hair grown yeti-length like. Yet, we also want to believe still that some form of a wild child exits; one before language, reason, and logic infected our spirits.

What is the antidote to this unfulfilled desire? How do we live with our current definition of what is human from now on? Who decides what will become of these creatures? Are we present day humans disturbing the ecosystem of the Idyll-Beast? Do you stalk, leave it alone, observe from a distance, trap—what's to be done? The ball is in the court of the visitor to Idyllwild if they see a sighting. One's reaction will be a sign of one's moral character.

Bigfoot, as a larger cultural phenomenon, makes periodic appearances in popular media. In the past twenty-five years, a small sampling includes the comedy film *Harry and the Hendersons* (1987) and subsequent TV series of the same name (1991-1993), about a family who adopt a Bigfoot called Harry. Eventually, the creature's existence is exposed, but despite the family's fear that he would be taken by the government, he was embraced by the public and achieves some fame.

More recently in 2011, the cable channel Animal Planet, created the documentary series, *Finding Bigfoot*. The show follows Matt Moneymaker, president of the Bigfoot Field Researchers Organization, and three sidekicks as they investigate Bigfoot sightings all over the country, not just in the Pacific Northwest— the traditional stomping ground in our folk imagination. For the most part, the crew records only grainy, night vision images of other animals and distance sounds that are interpreted as Bigfoot calls. Perhaps the crew will come to Idyllwild?

This past April 2012, production began on the film, *Exists*, headed by *Blair Witch Project* director Eduardo Sanchez. The film follows a group of twentysomethings who take a trip to a cabin deep in the wooded wilderness and are methodically hunted by a Bigfoot-like beast. In a recent issue of "Variety" magazine, Sanchez says, "The film is the first in a trilogy exploring and reinventing the Bigfoot myth." He goes on to say, "We all remember the terror of watching such classics as *The Legend of Boggy Creek*, and I look forward to making Bigfoot scary again."

For me, *Harry and the Hendersons* represents an attempt to domesticate or suburbanize the beast, but twenty-five years later, the beast has been returned back to the woods in our imagination, open to be stalked by cameras again, as if hunting grounds have been restocked with deer—as if the American frontier has once again been closed. But, *Exists* takes the retreat further. Sanchez's desire to make Bigfoot "scary again" is a further distancing from our human nature. He makes the animal side of ourselves not only beastly but monstrous and terrifying, positioning us as the prey rather than the hunter. But of course we are only hunting down ourselves.

The Idyll-Beast is a rebuttal to the modern world, creating doubt about the path we've taken that seems to be heading towards singularity in which human and machine will merge. It is a reminder that we live with amnesia also, as if we cannot remember who we are really, or at least an important part of ourselves. It lingers out there in the woods, so close yet so far. It will never be part of our lives until we remember that we must find another way to live with the rest of the animals and the plants on the earth, although we try our utmost to deny this membership with a prankster's smirk. Idyllwild is not a "Jurassic Park," but perhaps it could be considered "Feral Park," a tourist zone for our imagination to reconnect with the primal.

One day, I may walk into the woods of Idyllwild, where my clothes will be ripped off by branches, my hair will grow long, my feet will swell from exposure (hence, the name Bigfoot) and, before I know it, little tourist children will see me in the distance, drinking from a stream, then run to their day tripper parents, both excited and scared, yelling, "It's the Idyll-Beast!"

I may never see the Idyll-Beast, Bigfoot, or Sasquatch, but I'm grateful that the creature is embedded in our cultural imagination as a counterweight to living in a right-angled, urban world. The lasting impression that this unseen creature leaves is more a question, which asks: Civilization needs the Idyll-Beast, but does the beast need us? □

Lewis deSoto & Erin Neff: *Tahquitz*

(2012) (with Lewis deSoto)

Lewis deSoto & Erin Neff: Tahquitz is a site-specific installation using sound and light technology that animates the majestic forty-foot atrium of UCR's Culver Center of the Arts. "Tahquitz" (pronounced tah-kwish) is the name of a primordial creature, a *nukatem,* part of the creation story of the Cahuilla people who live in the Southern California areas of Palm Springs, San Gorgonio Pass, Hemet and Anza Borrego. This primordial being, according to the Cahuilla, wanders in the San Jacinto mountain range where a peak is named for him.

In the mid 1990s, Lewis deSoto presented an installation work with the same title, commissioned by Martin Friedman and Adam Weinberg of the American Center in Paris and the Denver Art Museum. This earlier version of *Tahquitz* is now in the collection of The Museum of Contemporary Art, Los Angeles. In creating another version for Culver Center of the Arts, deSoto has come back to this story in collaboration with mezzo-soprano Erin Neff, who lends her study of the Cahuilla language and her abilities as a composer/singer to the project. In the past, the artists have worked together in 2009 on *KLAGE* (Lament) a the San Jose Institute of Contemporary Art, San Jose, California, and in 2002 on *Haunt* (Cantus) at Wave Hill in Bronx, New York.

The peak that is named after Tahquitz, which is to the Cahuilla a sacred place, is represented by a large, eight-foot diameter, roughly shaped boulder that hangs just above a viewer's head in the atrium. Although it is one constructed by a theatrical prop house, there is a sense of gravity and weight that evokes the presence of Tahquitz's dwelling place. Additionally, it is a reminder of the dry desert location where Tahquitz exists and the reality of living in such a harsh environment, as well as an embodiment of endless hunger and desire, whether by the primordial being, craving for other life energies, or as commentary on today's society.

deSoto has installed an enormous translucent map of Tahquitz's location, the San Jacinto Mountain range, across the glass grid of the magnificent glass skylight that lights the Culver Atrium. This map, derived from a USGS map printed in the early 1900s, reverses gravity: one is at once below the map and floating above the land. It suggests that the world has been turned topsy-turvy literally as you enter into the timeless space of Tahquitz. As if told by a Cahuilla, you may become so disoriented as to be unable to leave and return to your family and friends.

On the backside of the atrium's open space there is a large light projection of a Cahuilla basket pattern that is slowly rotating. Made graphic and enlarged, the spinning design suggests that of a spiral galaxy too, as if to remind the viewer of the cosmic order of things referenced in everyday details of utilitarian objects, such as baskets.

On an antique table, opposite the boulder, there is an Edison cylinder phonograph from the early 1900s. It is a similar to the kind used for recording Cahuilla Bird Singers in 1918 by anthropologist Lucille Hooper. These recordings reside at UC

Berkeley's Phoebe A. Hearst Museum of Anthropology and in the Smithsonian's collections. The inclusion of both the phonograph and the USGS map from the early 1900s is also fitting as they connect with the installation's site at Culver Center, a building built originally in 1895 as a department store. The phonograph recording represents also the first time that the sound of another culture could be captured. It also points to how the technology used to record a culture can shape our views, whether that be framed by the two-minute limit of the wax cylinder, the scratchiness of its recording, or which native cultures and songs were selected for dissemination and thus given more importance over others.

There are four zones of sound in the installation. They are created with "audio spotlight" technology that allow for laser-like, precise aiming of sound. As one enters the space, in alignment with the boulder and the recorder down the center of the atrium, the sound of Cahuilla Elder Alvino Siva telling the story of Tahquitz in English and Cahuilla is heard. Standing under the boulder, one hears the sound of Erin Neff, singing a rendition of Siva's stories. If one passes into the zone of the Edison phonograph, one hears the sounds of *Tahquitz* vocalized by Lewis deSoto and Erin Neff, and then the 1918 Hooper recordings of the Bird Singers is heard. Otherwise, the room feels quiet for anyone not in these specific zones. The effect is not unlike hearing something "inside one's head" and is an uncanny, unexpected experience. In effect, it is as though the primordial being, Tahquitz, is talking to you, and perhaps ensnaring you, beginning the process of absorbing your life energy.

Neff sings three verses of song that are, essentially, an abridged version of the story as told by Alvino Siva. She transcribed the story in its original Cahuilla, before beginning her composition, in order to become attuned to its rhythmic and percussive nature, as she felt that getting the natural cadence of the Cahuilla had to be foremost in the composition. The text was then set to melodies she developed from music samples notated in Hansjakob Seiler's recording of Cahuilla spoken word stories, *Cahuilla Texts with an Introduction* (1970). The "voice" of Tahquitz was based on other written stories where it is noted that when Tahquitz makes his approach he makes the sounds "toooov" and "tevvvv." This recording was made in a place with resonant, hard surfaces so as to replicate the acoustic feeling of the giant rock in the San Jacinto Mountains that is Tahquitz's home and is where the Indian maiden was forced to live with Tahquitz.

Neff sings alternately as narrator, Indian maiden, Tahquitz, and fellow tribesman whose spirit has been stolen and consumed by Tahquitz's deep appetite for the life energies of other living beings. She also sings the complex story of a maiden who is kidnapped and held within his lair: a home inside a seemingly solid boulder on the mountain. She is made to live as he does: consuming the spirits of others. Finally, after much pleading, she is released back into the world and back to her village. After much cajoling she tells the story after having her neighbors build her a house. She perishes after the telling of the forbidden story.

In addition to the Tahquitz installation in the Culver
Center's central atrium, there are long tables and video monitors in
the North Atrium Gallery that display a variety of books and videos
about Lewis deSoto's past projects and Cahuilla culture. One can
also experience through video documentation the Erin Neff
contributions in *Cantus* and *Klage* (Lament).

For deSoto, Tahquitz continues his overriding exploration
into the history of how humans have come to think the universe
came to exist and operates, whether that is through religious,
mythic, or scientific avenues, or a combination of all three. But they
are all paths that suggest we look at the world through a language
of some sort. In this light, Tahquitz reflects on the legend of the
primordial being as existing in reality and through the retelling of
his existence through the Cahuilla language. The exhibition perhaps
asks how do this telling, this naming, and this lens of language,
reform Tahquitz when told in English and when sung by an opera
singer trained in European languages, though in concert with
Cahuilla Bird Singers.

deSoto's fascination with transformation of sacred
landscapes can be found in a seminal, early, photo-based project,
created just out of graduate school, and exhibited at UCR's
California Museum of Photography, *The Tahualtapa Project*, 1983-
1988. Its name refers to "The Hill of the Ravens" in Cahuilla lore.
The mountain in the San Bernardino Valley was later known as Mt.
Slover, and for nearly twelve decades, the presence of the
California Portland Cement plant in Colton, not far from Riverside,
mined limestone and used 3,000-degree kilns to turn it into clinker

bricks, and then ground the clinker into cement powder. It was the first such producer of cement in the United States. For this project, deSoto employed in his photographs a running motif that represented the outline of the once existing mountain. In essence, the project explored the theme of how a sacred mountain was transformed by both renaming it and grinding it down into the materials for the cities of a different kind of civilization.

However, this is not to say that although Tahualtapa has been transformed into cement, or that Tahquitz's dwelling place is represented by a prop boulder, or the songs about his travails are recorded for non-natives to hear, there is always spiritual power in everything. Objects are not dead but alive, and should therefore be approached not only with curiosity, but respect. Or as Lewis deSoto said in a recent lecture on his work at Culver Center, "Everyday objects have energy too. They can be power objects that carry an idea forward. Nothing is anonymous and everything is authored."

☐

Resurrection Machines of Ancient Egypt in San Bernardino and of Ancient Cinema in Hollywood

(2012)

The Sun rises in the East each morning and sets in the West each afternoon. I will die some day. Everyone will die at some point. The sun and death are common denominators. I drive towards the sun on the 215-North from Riverside, as if it is a beacon, not just a life giving star, but a magical amulet hanging in the sky or a god passing overhead. It is precisely these sentiments that motivate my journey to California State University San Bernardino's Robert V. Fullerton Museum of Art.

Remnants of ancient Egyptian's resurrection machines are on display there: amulets, statues of gods and goddesses, fragments of mummies, earthenware, all inscribed with hieroglyphics that helped deceased pharaohs and the wealthy navigate the underworld, ruled by Osiris.

The all-important sun-god, Ra, who ruled during the day, disappeared into this underworld at night, and in effect was resurrected each morning. Preparations to survive this underworld permeated ancient Egyptian life. Otherwise, the worse case scenario for both deities and humans is that the sun, or Ra, would not be reborn. Chaos would then set in and the fragile civilization along the banks of the Nile in Northern Africa would collapse.

Since life was saturated with the dualities of day and night, death and life, all in a cycle of birth and rebirth, most any object or writing was religious in nature and was meant to maintain balance in the universe, bringing order to chaos. This is perhaps most evident in the geography of the region: rich, fertile soil along the banks of the Nile was where life thrived, but each side of the Nile was flanked by a harsh, vast, barren desert that kept enemies at bay, but also meant death for anyone who ventured too far into the region. The image that populates every aspect of ancient Egyptian material culture is of the pharaoh, the intermediary between the mortal and divine worlds, working with the gods and goddesses on behalf of Egypt to hold back chaos.

Their modern day collector, W. Benson Harer, a former resident of San Bernardino, donated many of his pieces to CSUSB and others are on loan from his private collection. His collection is said to be one of the best in California. The pieces range in age from 4,000 B.C.—before the first pyramids were built—to about 500 A.D., after the decline of Egyptian dynastic rule and the transition into the periods of Greco-Roman rule, with the last hieroglyphic inscription in 394 A.D., eventually falling under Islamic rule in 641 A.D. The death knell to the survivability of ancient Egyptian culture and its various deities was, after coming under the rule of Rome, when Christianity was eventually declared the official religion.

Perhaps it is the cultural and religious dualities of ancient Egypt that were attractive to Harer, a retired obstetrician and gynecologist, a position that focused on bringing new life in the world, while his collection of ancient Egyptian artifacts focused on the afterlife.

Intimacy with Funerary Objects

Although there are no intact, full-size mummies nor a plethora of golden artifacts, as in the two traveling exhibitions of King Tut's tomb contents, which came to Los Angeles County Museum of Art in 1978 and most recently, again, in 2005, the collection's display at CSUSB provides an opportunity to be away from crowds and an intimate view of the parts in the resurrection-machine-stone-tombs that helped ancient Egyptians survive their journey in the afterlife.

Mummification became important because the body was the shelter to which the pharaoh's *ba* and *ka* spirits returned. But the body had to look as familiar as it did when alive in this world so that these spirits could find there way back, hence, preservation of the body through mummification, the numerous hieroglyphic inscriptions that announces the deceased's name, and the painting of their likenesses on coffin lids that covered the wrapped mummies.

Relative to mummification, highlights in the CSUSB collection include a set of four canopic jars from the Third Intermedia Period (1069-664 B.C.). They are made of limestone with black ink inscriptions in hieratic Egyptian, a writing style that developed alongside hieroglyphics but written with brush and ink rather than carved.

During mummification, five internal organs were removed from the body and embalmed. Only the heart, believed to be the center of intellect and emotions, was returned to the body. The other four organs were stored in canopic jars placed in the tomb near the body. According to a CSUSB wall label, the jars, used from the Old Kingdom through the Greco-Roman times, evolved from simple, undecorated containers to inscribed vases with lids carved in the shape of the heads of the fours sons of Horus. Each of these minor deities guarded one of the organs and was represented by an animal important to ancient Egyptians: falcon for intestines, jackal for stomach, human for liver, and baboon for lungs.

Another nice piece is a Winged Scarab Pectoral, from some time between the 21st and 24th dynasties (1069-715 B.C.), and made from faience, or glazed earthenware. Pectorals of various types were often placed on a mummy's breast. This example shows a winged scarab beetle, a powerful symbol of Ra's, or the sun's daily rebirth. The scarab is modeled on the dung beetle, who rolls a dung ball, where it lays eggs that turn into larva and eat from the dung, thus, the cycle of death and life is embodied, and reinforced with the sphere of the dung suggesting the round, life-giving sun. Each section is pierced to allow it to be stitched to the exterior of the mummy wrappings.

Other items on view include a coffin lid, a mummified hand with blue faience rings poking through the wraps, and even items towards the end of ancient Egyptian culture that reveal aesthetic influences from when it came under the rule of Persia, Greece, and Rome at varying times. For example, the curly hairstyle of Grecians, often seen in their statues, is evident in several small busts at the end of the exhibition's chronological layout.

Egyptomania

In Europe and America, Egyptomania took hold in the nineteenth century as a result of French Emperor Napoleon Bonaparte's campaign into Egypt and Syria (1798-1801). Later, Howard Carter, an English archaeologist and Egyptologist, and his discovery in 1922 of 14th-century BC pharaoh Tutankhamen's tomb fueled the imagination. The influence of these discoveries are evident in a short list of Western architecture: the pyramids at The Luxor Hotel in Las Vegas, the glass pyramid that serves as an entrance to Paris' Louvre Museum, the Washington Monument's obelisk shape and, locally, Hollywood's Egyptian Theater.

The Egyptian Theater, which opened two weeks prior to Carter's announced discovery on November 2, 1922, was designed with exterior and interior walls that contain Egyptianesque painted figures and hieroglyphics. There are also four immense columns that flank the main entrance, rising twenty feet high. Sid Grauman, who also opened the Chinese Theater in 1927, further west on Hollywood Boulevard, built it. However, Grauman's Chinese Theater developed its own take on immortality—celebrity handprints, footprints, and signatures impressed into sections of cement throughout the theater's forecourt—that eventually overshadowed the Egyptian. After falling in disrepair through the decades, the City of Los Angeles sold it for a dollar to the American

Cinematheque, with the caveat that the organization restores it to its former, architectural glory days. It reopened to the public on December 4, 1998 and has been showing an adventuresome film program since then.

In light of my travel to San Bernardino to view ancient Egyptian artifacts and considering The Egyptian Theater and cinema's intertwined history with philosophical thoughts about immortality—whether via mummification or cinemafication—I consider that the projected light onto the theater screen, enveloping me while I sit in a cool, tomb-like temperature, is a representation of the sun god, Ra, and his cycle of life and death each day and night.

Each time the same film is projected, the sun "rises" within the theater, and thus the chaos of the world is abated. Actors, possessing pharaoh-like status in our twenty-first century culture, are resurrected too so that they may live on and become gods and goddesses eventually.

Perhaps ancient Egyptians were the first filmmakers in the most rudimentary since of depicting a succession of pictures—in the form of hieroglyphs--that add up to a narrative. As I walk among the artifacts at CSUSB and survey the hieroglyphs on the stela or coffin lid, they are redolent of filmstrips and their successive celluloid frames, at least prior to their own death as they fade into the underworld, replaced by a new god, *Digital Ra.*

There is one location in Hollywood today that appears to bring together the living and the dead before the resurrection machine of cinema—the Hollywood Forever Cemetery. In fact, it is located not too far from the Egyptian Theater on Sunset Boulevard.

Founded in 1899, the cemetery was an integral part of the growth of early Hollywood. Paramount Studios was built on the back half of the original Hollywood Cemetery, where the studio is still in operation today. The cemetery of choice for most of the founders of Hollywood's great studios, Hollywood Forever Cemetery is now listed on the National Register of Historic Sites. Its new owners have transformed it into a hip gathering spot over the past decade, most notably featuring rock concerts and a film series called Cinespia, showing past Hollywood classics such as *Sunset Boulevard* and *Scarface*. As for the buried Hollywood royalty, visitors come from all over the world to pay respects to Johnny Ramone, Jayne Mansfield, Rudolph Valentino, Douglas Fairbanks, and Cecil B. DeMille.

Towards the Setting Sun

I leave the campus of CSU San Bernardino, heading back towards Riverside, in the direction of the western coast where the sun is setting. Ra is disappearing into the underworld. I can only hope that he will rise tomorrow morning.

But, perhaps, I will keep heading towards the sun until I come to Pacific Coast Highway. I will then turn right to head north on PCH, until I arrive three hours later in the small, coastal town of Guadalupe, south of San Luis Obispo. It is there that archaeologists, film historians, and Egyptologists can converge with common interests.

Buried in the beach sand is an ancient Egyptian city from 1923, one year after Howard Carter's King Tut tomb discovery. Resting within the Nipomo sand dunes are the plaster remnants from Cecil B. DeMille's 1923 silent movie *The Ten Commandments*. Instead of removing the set after filming, as it would have been too expensive, the crew simply buried it some ninety years ago— ancient history in cinema history.

The original set had an Avenue of the Sphinxes, with twenty, five-ton statues lining the sides. There were also four, forty-ton statues of the Pharaoh Ramses II, each three stories high. The city was protected by an 80-foot-wide, 120-foot-tall wall covered with hieroglyphics modeled on those found a year earlier in King Tut's Tomb. In 1983, a group of determined film buffs-- inspired by a cryptic clue in DeMille's posthumously published autobiography--located the remains of the set.

Near the beach entrance, there is a small museum with some of the plaster artifacts. It is there mainly to prevent people from searching among the dunes for the foot of one of the tumbled three story high pharaoh statues. In fact, the whereabouts of known artifacts is kept secret in order to protect these sacred objects.

When I visited the Guadalupe Nipomo Dunes Visitor Center a few years ago, I was able to handle some of the crumbling plaster remnants. They were silent like the silent film for which they were props. And like the Book of the Dead, inscribed in hieroglyphics on the tomb walls of pharaohs to help them navigate the underworld, these ninety-year old artifacts linked me to cinema, today's resurrection machines. What movie will I watch tomorrow so that the sun will rise again and so that I will then live another day? Perhaps it will be DeMille's version of Moses leading the Israelites to the Promised Land on the shores of the California coast. Ancient Egypt fell to the Romans and the Romans fell to Hollywood.

☐

An Inland Empire Afterlife: The Immortality Project, Cryonics, and a 26-Foot Tall Marilyn Monroe

(2012)

Is death the end of life or a gateway to a hereafter? Millions of people have reported near-death and out-of-body experiences in the last century alone. For millennia, major religions such as Christianity and Islam have promoted the existence of an afterlife. Literature, religious texts, and anecdotes are brimming with stories of reincarnation, resurrection, and immortality. Yet, despite their influence on cultural habits that sometime lead to both inspired utopian communities but also to persecution of others, there has been no comprehensive and rigorous, scientific study of global reports about near-death and other experiences, or of how belief in immortality influences human behavior. That will change with the award of a three-year, $5 million grant by the John Templeton Foundation to John Martin Fischer, distinguished professor of philosophy at the University of California, Riverside, to undertake a rigorous examination of a wide range of issues related to immortality. The John Templeton Foundation, located near Philadelphia, supports research on subjects ranging from complexity, evolution and infinity to creativity, forgiveness, love, and free will.

"We will be very careful in documenting near-death experiences and other phenomena, trying to figure out if these offer plausible glimpses of an afterlife or are biologically induced illusions," Fischer said. "Our approach will be uncompromisingly scientifically rigorous. We're not going to spend money to study alien-abduction reports. We will look at near-death experiences and try to find out what's going on there — what is promising, what is nonsense, and what is scientifically debunked. We may find something important about our lives and our values, even if not glimpses into an afterlife." The Immortality Project will promote collaborative research between scientists, philosophers and theologians. A major goal will be to encourage interdisciplinary inquiry into the family of issues relating to immortality — and how these bear on the way we conceptualize our own lives.

Cryonics In Riverside

It is perhaps not so strange that studies in immortality would be centered in Riverside. The city was once the location for Alcor, one of the leading organizations to promote cryonics, that is, a preservation technique for damaged bodies that cannot be sustained by more traditional medical methods. By preserving the body now, the hope is that technology will advance to a point in the future whereby the body can be resuscitated. The underlying notion is a spark of "life" still exists despite legal and medical definitions of death.

In the 1960s Robert Ettinger founded the cryonics (cryonic hibernation) movement and authored *The Prospect of Immortality*. An inspiration for many like-minded people, his book covered the practical, legal, ethical, and moral impact of freezing and reviving human beings. Mainly, he wanted to layout a scientific and technological argument in order to dispel misleading notions of the process, such as those depicted in horror and sci-fi B movies.

In 1972, Fred and Linda Chamberlain incorporated Alcor as the Alcor Society for Solid State Hypothermia in the State of California. According to organizational history on the company's website, it was on July 16, 1976 that Alcor performed its first human cryopreservation. Alcor grew slowly in its early years. The organization counted only 50 members in 1985, which was the year it cryopreserved its third patient. In 1986 some of Alcor's members formed Symbex, a small investment company that funded a building in Riverside, California, for lease by Alcor, which moved from Fullerton, California to the new building in Riverside in 1987.

In one case history related to Riverside, on May 8, 1988, a long-time cryonicist and Alcor member, Bob (referred to by his first name only in order to protect the privacy of the member's family) was placed into whole-body cryonic suspension at Alcor's Riverside, California facility. The patient was a 72-year-old man with a long history of arteriosclerosis and congestive heart failure. There is a fascinating account of the procedures on the Alcor website. Excerpts from it are listed below in chronological order from his arrival at the Riverside facility to his final encapsulation in the cryogenic housing unit:

An hour and 25 minutes after his arrival in the facility, surgery to open Bob's chest and connect him to the heart-lung machine was begun. The surgery to cannulate Bob's aorta and right heart for blood washout and cryoprotective perfusion proved enormously difficult. Bob's chest was a mass of adhesions and scars from two previous bypass operations.

At 2:14 AM on the morning of May 9, blood washout commenced. Washout proceeded with extreme difficulty due to the massive clotting that was present. Initially the right atrium was left open to allow large clots to be vented into the operative field and sucked out (along with draining venous perfusate) with a wide-bore suction line. Once the largest of these clots were expelled, a standard venous return cannula was placed in the right heart and perfusion was continued.

At 4:37 AM cryoprotective perfusion began using a 5% glycerol solution in the new sucrose-HEPES perfusate. Hydroxyethyl starch was present in 5% concentration as the colloid (used to minimize fluid accumulation (edema) between cells). The cryoprotective ramp was begun at 4:41 AM.

At 10:15 AM, ice packs were removed from Bob and he was placed inside two large plastic bags. He was then submerged in a tank of silicone oil (Silcool) which had been precooled to -10°C.

By maintaining a 10°C to 15°C differential between surface and core temperatures, Bob was slowly cooled to -79°C over the next 35 hours by gradual addition of dry ice to the Silcool bath.

On Thursday, May 12, a team of Alcor members...assembled at the facility to transfer Bob from dry ice to liquid nitrogen storage. The Alcor dual-patient cryogenic dewar was rocked into horizontal position after being precooled to approximately -100°C. The metal tank used for Silcool/dry ice cooling (and now drained of Silcool and completely filled with dry ice) was lifted out of its insulating container and transferred to two rolling dollies so that it could be wheeled into position in the central work area of the facility.

On May 17th, the dewar housing Bob was filled to the top with liquid nitrogen and Bob entered long term cryogenic storage. He remains submerged in liquid nitrogen in the Alcor facility in Riverside -- waiting.

By 1990 Alcor had grown to 300 members. In response to concerns that the California facility was too small and vulnerable to earthquake risk, the organization purchased a building in Scottsdale, Arizona in 1993 and moved its patients to it in 1994.

Frozen Disney

The source of one of the most persistent urban legends associated with cryogenics is in Anaheim, an hour's drive south of Riverside, in Orange County. The most notable person to be unknowingly associated with cryogenics was Walt Disney, who died on December 15, 1966. Over the decades, the rumor has persisted that Disney arranged for the cryopreservation of his body under Disneyland's "Pirates of the Caribbean," waiting the day when he will be resurrected and perhaps create an additional amusement park—Zombie Land.

Part of the fuel behind the rumors of his possible interest in resurrection via yet to come technology could have been Disney's association with imagining the future in his Disneyland attractions, which would have included, at the time, the monorail and Tomorrowland. Additionally, there were the animatronic, life-size figures speaking and moving as if practicing for the day when they will be free-thinking robots after a human brain transplant or receiving downloaded mind-data, depending on which technology is developed first.

This legend is so strong that the location of his frozen body is a guessing game. After CalArts opened in Valencia, California in 1971, it was rumored that his body was ensconced there in a basement. In the early 1990s, two art students Burt Payne and Steve Hillenberg were inspired to create the Frozen Walt Doll. Along with being a commentary on Hollywood myth-making, the first two editions, Black Tie and Red Tie, supposedly financed their $10, 000 annual tuition education at CalArts.

A Cinematic Meaning of Life

Contemplating the possible avenues of inquiry with The Immortality Project, John Fisher says, "if you believe we exist as immortal beings, you could ask how we could survive death as the very same person in an afterlife. If you believe in reincarnation, how can the very same person exist if you start over with no memories?"

According to a press announcement from UCR about Fisher's initiative, other questions philosophers may consider are: Is immortality potentially worthwhile or not? Would existence in an afterlife be repetitive or boring? Does death give meaning to life? Could we still have virtues like courage if we knew we couldn't die? What can we learn about the meaning of our lives by thinking about immortality?

The last question in this litany is a striking one. One answer is brought strikingly to the forefront in another Inland Empire city, Palm Springs.

Forever Marilyn, a 26-foot-tall statue of the late actress was erected there this past May, after being on view in Chicago. It is located at Palm Canyon and Tahquitz Canyon Way, where it will remain until June 2013.

The sculpture by Seward Johnson, the 80-year-old artist and Johnson & Johnson heir who's known for casting famous images into giant sculptures, re-created the scene from the 1955 film "The Seven Year Itch" in which a drafty New York subway grate lifts Monroe's skirt to tantalizing heights.

Attention around the statue heated up this August, as it is the 50th anniversary of Monroe's death, who was born 86 years ago, on June 1, 1926, and died Aug. 5, 1962. Anyone looking to find accidental connections between disparate events might view the press announcement of Fisher's Immortality Project on July 31st, five days before Monroe's anniversary death, as uncannily coincidental for Inland Empire afterlife-aficionados.

But, back to Fisher's question relative to Monroe's out-sized memorial, "What can we learn about the meaning of our lives by thinking about immortality?" Or, to rephrase the last few words, "...by thinking about Marilyn Monroe's immortality?"

Marco Brambilla is a bi-coastal, contemporary artist who has perhaps best answered this re-engineered question.

In his 2011 survey exhibition at the Santa Monica Museum of Art, he included *Evolution (Megaplex)*. It is the second in a series of large-scale video collages and the first of his works to be executed in stereoscopic 3D. The history of humankind is illustrated as a vast scrolling video mural depicting the spectacle of human conflict across time through the lens of cinematic genres such as science fiction, war, and western films. The prior work was *Civilization* (2008) that presented a satirical take on the concepts of eternal punishment and celestial reward. Brambilla's process involves looping hundreds of individual channels of video that are blended into an ever-evolving landscape. In much of his work, there is the feeling of moving from the depths of hell to the gates of heaven, all the while making a sly commentary on the pomposity of big-budget "epic" films, whether they come from directors Cecil B. DeMille a century ago or James Cameron today.

Perhaps then there will still be tunnels of light reported by near-death returnees, but instead of greeting other deceased family members or angels, it will really be more like sitting in a movie theater in which the figures at the end of the tunnel are our favorite actors. In other words, Brambilla may suggest that even Hollywood's relentless entertainment industry will have seeped into our most personal experience—death. Your body will die alone but in the afterlife your spirit will sit with other fans watching your favorite movie—over and over.

Life is Death

A less cynical response to Fisher's question that asks "what we can learn about the meaning of our lives by thinking about immortality," would suggest that despite the best efforts by Alcor or fans of a frozen, youthful image of what would now be a fifty-year old corpse, is that we still fear death quite a bit.

It is still very hard to believe that after emerging from so very little as organisms, and then achieving a level of self-awareness that has allowed us to land a rover on Mars in early August (nicely coincidental with the timing of the announcement of The Immortality Project and Monroe's anniversary death), that we will then die.

Freezing bodies and erecting gargantuan statues of dead celebrities are strategies for fleeing from the reality of death that will fail. However, these schemes are not unique to our lifetime. Ancient Egyptian artifacts can be found just a few miles north of Riverside at California State University San Bernardino's Robert Fullerton Museum that are reminders of early attempts to freeze, or mummify, bodies over six-thousand years ago. The mammoth crucifix atop Mount Rubidoux in the heart of Riverside and its related Easter Sunrise service (that has been in effect since 1909) is a reminder of how belief in resurrection permeates Western culture via Christian tales.

What we do know is that life precedes death. So, to fear death is to find failure in a life that did not prepare us for leaving that which is familiar in this particular, waking world. So, perhaps, one way to not fear death, and therefore, to reconsider concepts of immortality, is not to fear life. Then, our society may become less anxious over death's unknowns. Perhaps Bob will be resuscitated in his new Alcor quarters but will he feel any less anxious about having to die again? ☐

Hell's Union: Motorcycle Club Cuts as American Folk Art

(2012)

Collected by artist and motorcycle rider Jeff Decker, *Hell's Union: Motorcycle Club Cuts as American Folk Art* is an exhibition at UCR ARTSblock that features defunct motorcycle club "cuts," or vests, and their assorted, colorful club "colors," or patches, that represent a unique form of American folk art embodying the freedom and nonconformity symbolized by bikers. Jeff Decker is an artist famed for his bronze sculptures of vintage motorcycles and he grew up surrounded by the car culture of southern California in the 1960s. The cuts in this show are almost all denim and are from the 60s and 70s.

Decker had the insight to look at the cuts as American folk art rather than only as artifacts of mythologized outlaw motorcycle clubs. As he said during a walkthrough at the exhibition's reception, "I don't look at the cuts as anything clandestine. To me, it is folk art that has been ignored."

With this notion, the cuts may be viewed in the same context of Amish quilts that use their own set of "colors" that emphasize solids and simple compositions, but fine craftsmanship. Like a MC president and founder, their local religious leaders approve their "colors" too.

Carrying "colors" began with the military. The most familiar are the medieval European armies in which standards were carried with a coat of arms. Up until industrial warfare that began in the twentieth century, which allowed for some distance from the enemy, it was important to know the whereabouts of one's regiment and how to keep formation when smoke and dirt were in the air, much less the chaos of charging and falling bodies. Its importance is underscored by the fact that experienced soldiers, or flag guards, were assigned to its protection. So, to protect one's flag or an attempt to capture an enemy's "colors" were both great feats of combat. Now, more symbolic that tactical, but for the same reason, it is why MC's go to such lengths to protect their "colors." In today's American culture, in which success and happiness are often defined by money, their fierce protection might also be viewed as protecting one's "brand," akin to a "cease-and-desist" letter sent on a top-notch lawyer's letterhead to a perceived copyright infringer.

The cuts are from defunct motorcycle clubs (MC) primarily. You will not find a Hell's Angel cut. This is due to the fact that "colors," or the patches, have to be earned. No one can wear the colors unless they go through a right of passage. Decker says that in this respect, younger riders often question his motivations, mainly because he did not go through their various rights of passages in the clubs represented. But, according to Decker, "the older guys get what I'm doing. In fact, they often say, 'Maybe you will tell the story right.'" Decker feels that Hunter S. Thompson was an excellent writer, for example, when he published his 1967 book *Hell's Angels: The Strange and Terrible Saga of the Outlaw Motorcycle Gangs*, but he was still an outsider. And then the insiders are not the most articulate. So there is no well-written history yet, at least this is

Decker's sentiment. At this point, his respect for the cuts, and his manner of displaying them in their own, deeply shadowboxed, black frames, as if they are religious reliquaries, is one way to begin to tell the story visually.

Decker's collection focuses on cuts from the 1960s and 70s. From hearing him talk, my sense is that the reasons are varied: connection to his childhood when his father worked on cars, and even having a chance to hang around Kustum Kulture car customizer God, Ed "Big Daddy" Roth; and because there were so many films at the time that played on the fears of small town American: invasion and take over by a foreign menace, whether it be aliens from outer space, Communist Russians, or lawless bike gangs. I think that perhaps Decker would like to rectify a bit the suburban fantasies of ancient Vikings coming to pillage and rape as depicted in *The Wild Angeles* (1966) with Peter Fonda and Bruce Dern, which was followed by *Devil's Angels* (1967), starring actor-director John Cassavetes; Jack Nicholson in *Hells Angels on Wheels* (1967); *The Glory Stompers* (1968), starring Dennis Hopper, *The Cycle Savages* (1969), starring Bruce Dern, or a plethora of other biker-related films available to stream on Netflix in one's own subdivision of the mind. After starring in this new genre of B-movies, Fonda, Hopper, and Nicholson collaborated in 1969 on *Easy Rider*, a conversion of the violent motorcycle gang movie into one for the hippies.

In fact, it is these biker-ploitation films that contributed to a decline in sales of "machines" which led, in part, to the American Motorcycle Association (AMA) distancing themselves from certain

MCs. In essence, in the United States, clubs became an outlaw one because of not being sanctioned by the AMA, which included not following their rules, and subsequently making up their own bylaws. Then the AMA supposedly made a comment, although denied by the AMA, which distinguished them as representing 99% of riders in the U.S., most family-oriented, implying that there was a remaining, undesirable 1%. Of course, this designation was taken up as a matter of pride by the outlaw MCs, and is represented by a diamond shaped 1% patch on their cuts.

As a collector, Decker also seems attracted to the cut-sleeve cuts from the 60s and 70s because they are made from denim. The cotton fabric was particularly apt for absorbing urine, blood, and dirt, thus, capturing a patina of authenticity and individuality. Later, in the 1980s, MCs started wearing leather jackets because, in part, they were easier to clean, according to Decker. During a walkthrough at the opening reception for the exhibition someone asked about issues of preservation, as some of the cuts were barely intact. Jeff summed up both the badge of honor sensibility with the stains and unintended preservation, "They're pretty pickled already!" Despite meeting a collector's desire for authenticity, the more unwashed, overly mended, and greasier the shoulders from hair, the more the cut represented the wearers long-term commitment to the MC. It is for the same reasons that an appraiser on *Antiques Roadshow* will scold an owner who has scoured the patina off of a piece of centuries old furniture, as it may have provided protection over time, it removes its history through use and, for these reasons, reduces the market value considerably.

Reminiscing on his favorite cut in the show, Decker says, "I think Hell's Union is one of the strongest. Splattered bleach on it, leather fringe, military medals, police patches taken from police when pulled over. The back has great embroidery. It's my favorite for its aesthetic."

The general key to the placement of insignia goes something like the following. AMA club members generally wear only a single or two-piece patch, while the outlaw clubs wear three-piece patches. The top, curved "rocker" and central logo signify the club; the bottom rocker designates the chapter, such as the city or region, e.g. Frisco; an MC patch means "motorcycle club;" swastikas are there to offend but more in a punk rock, shock value way rather than as an in-depth political, neo-Nazi stance; "13" designates a pot smoker, with the "3" being an "M" on its side for marijuana; and then there are a myriad of other patches, like the 1% diamond.

The 1% designation represents, literally and symbolically, the super-rich in this country also. It is code too for an oligarchy of Wall Street corporations that would appear to run the "Main Streets" in the U.S. too; replacing invading aliens and Communists as a common enemy and affront to neighborly cooperation and regional collegiality. Initially, it may appear ironic that a caste of downtrodden outlaws considers themselves as 1% too. But perhaps there is little difference between the two, as both rule by fear: one through a new indebtedness and the other through physical violence. I make this extreme comparison because from an outsider's viewpoint, the cut, the colors, the insignia, the harsh manner by which respect is required and maintained, seem to be about creating conformity of the highest order. It is a uniform, after all. But, then, maybe this has been the impetus for what we call folk art today. When executed, it may not have been called art. Rather, it was a process e.g. the quilting circle, and an object that helped generate community cohesion by following both written and unwritten rules.

The degree of protocols is evident in an artifact on display in the exhibition. The "Death Barons Rules" were found folded up in the front, left pocket of the Death Baron cut. Forty rules are typewritten on the paper. There may have been more, but this one page provides insight into their organization and governance. Some highlights include:

- Rule #2: No leave of absence will be granted unless member is paid up in full all fines due and etc.
- Rule #7: If a member must leave the meeting early, he must have a good reason.
- Rule #11: If money is needed for emergencies resulting from club activity, each member will pay an equal amount.
- Rule #14: All members will show respect due to the officers at all times.
- Rule #15: Members will be expected to wear his colors at meetings, on trips, and when visiting with other clubs. At times other than these it will be up to the individual as to whether or not he wants to wear his colors.

- Rule #16: Any member may bring in a prospect providing he is a stand up person.
- Rule #22: After 10 pm, members will shut off, and start up their machines, beyond the driveway.
- Rule #25: Members will be allowed to bring their "old ladies" to the club house, except during business.
- Rule #26: No member shall desecrate colors.
- Rule #27: No member shall allow another member to be attacked, or harassed by anyone.
- Rule #28: No member shall allow anyone to wear his colors.
- Rule #33: Any member found not paying for refreshments will be fined $5.00.
- Rule #34: No member will sit on or handle another member's machine.
- Rule #35: All members will maintain an area residence, Fairfield, Stratford, Trumbull, Bridgeport, Milford, New Haven.
- Rule #38: All members must have machines of 500 c.c. or more.
- Rule #39: No member shall fight another unless both agree to take their colors off. If one member refuses to take his colors off the matter will be dropped, then and there.
- Rule #40: If one member insists on fighting the matter will be brought before the club and they will decide what will happen.

The impression is one of both household rules and of military-style regimentation in order to create solid unity. However, I do understand that organizational consistency can fulfill a desire for fraternity and camaraderie too. Admittedly, an MC is probably more like a family than their bloodline for many of the young men that were and are in clubs then and now.

The gist that I get from the reading the rules is one of an odd domesticity too. With this notion, I cannot help but want to see what the rules may be for a quilting club, that is, in light of considering the MC cuts as folk art, and considering folk art as less about rebellious expression and more about following the crowd, although visually. I've reviewed a variety of rules and bylaws for quilting clubs. Here are some highlights that parallel the excerpts from the Death Barons' bylaws:

- Article II, Purpose: Enhance community knowledge of all forms of quilt making, patterns, and the history of quilt making by providing general and educational meetings, fun and fellowship
- Article VI, Dues: Section 1. Annual dues shall be paid in full by the last meeting in January. After August 1, dues will be prorated. ▯▯Section 2. Proceeds from dues shall be used to defray costs of operating the club, which include reprographics materials, quilting supplies, goodwill gestures for members, and miscellaneous expenses incurred in annual social events. Proceeds may also be donated to other service projects as recommended by

Board and approved by a majority vote of the members present at a membership meeting. ⏹⏹Section 3. Upon disbandment of the Quilting Club, all monies in the treasury shall be distributed as selected by the membership at a special meeting called for this purpose.

- Rules
- The machines are to be used by those members enrolled in the class or activity only. All persons using the machines must be trained. The other portion of the room will be available to open sewing for members working on personal projects with permission from the Instructor only.
- DO NOT change the bottom bobbin tension on any machine.
- Everyone uses their own bobbins and supplies when using the machines. Bobbins and needles are available for purchase from the club officers. If it is a club project then supplies will be provided.
- Equipment and supplies belong to the club. These shall not be used for personal use. Some cupboards are locked for safekeeping and require a special key from an officer. Members who wish to make items to sell for profit cannot use Club equipment or supplies. (i.e. making items to sell at craft fairs, school fairs or in a member's employment.
- New members need to be trained on the use of the machines and how the sewing room operates, such as duties and checking out of books, selling of club items, etc.

Honestly, belonging to club with such overt rules and concern for conduct would be the last thing that I would want to do. It's why I would never want to live in a place with a homeowners association.

But, what if I were to venture into creating my own Riverside-based MC? I could harken back to the founding days of the Hells Angels in San Bernardino, just a few miles north of Riverside. The first Hells Angels Motorcycle Club was founded in the Fontana/San Bernardino area in 1948. The San Bernardino charter (also called "Berdoo") still exists, although most of its original members at one time moved northwards to Oakland. This removal is probably the reason why many outsiders wrongly describe Oakland as the Mother Charter of Hells Angels MC, which was founded by Sonny Barger.

Would an MC called "The Artists" find members?

From 1936 to 2003, Laguna Beach High School athletic teams were called the "Artists," in recognition of its reputation as an art colony. In 2003, the student body voted to call themselves the "Breakers," which was the name used for 19 months before the 1936 name change. The new name not only alludes to the breaking waves along the rocky shoreline but also sounds tougher. Maybe it was difficult to follow a standard emblazoned with a painter's palette?

In light of my profession, perhaps I'll go with creating an MC called "The Curators." It would reach back to the early 20th century when artists were reacting against the World Wars and the results of rapid industrialization, i.e. the Futurists and Dada.

The Futurists had a love of machines too, like the MCs represented in this exhibition. And, they too wanted the machines to help break the rules of institutions, such as the academies, libraries, and museums. Their adulation for the machine, war, and anything to disrupt a way of status quo thinking is akin to the MC's emphasis on motorcycles traversing the country as if there were no country, as if their tire prints in their dirt were redistricting the vote, and their upside down police badges next to swastikas were meant to challenge those who say, "You can't."

As if speaking to the disaffected youth of the 1950s, 60s, and up to today, F.T. Marinetti wrote in his 1909 Italian "Manifesto of Futurism": "Indeed daily visits to museums, libraries and academies (those cemeteries of wasted effort, cavalries of crucified dreams, registers of false starts!) is for artists what prolonged supervision by the parents is for intelligent young men, drunk with their own talent and ambition."

More excerpts from "Manifesto of Futurism" that share the same sentiments expressed by many outlaw MCs, artists, and nonconformists, and done so in manner that was/is meant to shock and not be politically correct:

- Literature has up to now magnified pensive immobility, ecstasy and slumber. We want to exalt movements of aggression, feverish sleeplessness, the double march, the perilous leap, the slap and the blow with the fist.
- We declare that the splendor of the world has been enriched by a new beauty: the beauty of speed. A racing

automobile with its bonnet adorned with great tubes like serpents with explosive breath ... a roaring motorcar which seems to run on machine-gun fire, is more beautiful than the Victory of Samothrace.

- Beauty exists only in struggle. There is no masterpiece that has not an aggressive character. Poetry must be a violent assault on the forces of the unknown, to force them to bow before man.
- We want to glorify war — the only cure for the world — militarism, patriotism, the destructive gesture of the anarchists, the beautiful ideas which kill, and contempt for woman.
- We want to demolish museums and libraries, fight morality, feminism and all opportunist and utilitarian cowardice.

A proposal for the design of my MC colors for The Curators of Riverside:

- Top Rocker: The Curators
- Middle Logo: Half of an apple joined to half of an orange, alluding to the phrase "apples and oranges" that is employed when acknowledging that two disparate elements have been forced into a comparison, but in this case, the forced juxtaposition is embraced as it generates new meanings, none of which is the absolute correct one
- Bottom Rocker: Riverside

- Patch #1: MC
- Patch #2: Infinity symbol, ∞, in order to represent engagement with ambiguity of meaning when analyzing objects, events, or people.

Some rules:

- All colors will be handmade and hand sewn in order to emphasize the rule of the hand over the machine; individual expression over crowdsourcing and polling.
- Cut-sleeve vests will be made from discarded painted canvases obtained from trash bins behind art schools.
- Every club discussion or challenge to an outsider will center on two questions: What is the context in which the object is situated or an event took place? What is the apparent intention of the object's maker or the event organizer / facilitator / instigator / agitator? □

Visiting with China's Ancient Terra Cotta Warriors, or Combat-Ready for Paradise

(2008)

Walking among funerary statues in *Terra Cotta Warriors: Guardians of China's First Emperor* at the Bowers Museum in Santa Ana, I reflect on war in the afterlife. Twenty figures are part of the display from the tomb of China's first emperor, Shi Huang Di (259-210 B.C.). He unified warring states and centralized the government. He would be known as the Emperor Qin, pronounced "chin"--this articulation considered the source for the country's designation by the West as "China."

For 38 years, Shi Huang Di assigned over 700,000 workers to build a mausoleum with life-size terra cotta warriors to protect him throughout eternity and to rule another empire while there. Discovered in 1974 by local farmers, they vary in height, averaging around six feet, the tallest being the generals. Warriors, chariots, horses, officials, acrobats, strongmen, and musicians are among the citizenry's effigies. Up to 8,000 life-size soldiers, 130 chariots with 520 horses and 150 cavalry horses were buried with him.

Varying facial expressions are one of the more unique characteristics of these two millennia old statues. Whether an archer or chariot driver, the studded plates of armor or the hairs of assorted mustaches, such details can be discerned today still. Their apparent individuality is a quality that makes each unsettling. I cannot but help fantasize that I will be caught amidst their awakening when sparked back into life. Perhaps this mystical act will be prompted by America's sitting mad sovereign; seizing upon this military presence in the "country of California" that lay west from his seat of muscle. Troop reinforcements are needed overseas.

After appreciating these statues that have been removed from an excavation site the size of an airplane hanger and encompassing Qin's necropolis in China's Shaanxi province, some 6300 miles away from Bowers Museum, I return to the freeway. It rises above Santa Ana like the Great Wall of China, also initiated by Qin.

Radio waves are soaked with news about cell phones and wires attached to batteries hanging on a belt of explosives. They wrap around a man's waist in another land that dates back to ancient Mesopotamia, cradle of civilization, 7600 miles away from L.A., cradle of celebrities. We're both commuting, but from two different deserts; mine the Mojave, his Syrian.

In the toll lane, I pass under a radar antenna that alerts a precision engineered, four-inch square plastic box affixed to my windshield to beep. It is a signal that a fee has been charged electronically to an account in an unknown location. I'm in the FasTrak lane now. My device being triggered is not his device—one activated by sacrifice.

Yellow, plastic pylons divide my FasTrak from the other four, standard lanes full of poor souls who constitute a sluggish congestion of cars moving unhurriedly. There are too many bumpers forming an armored millipede with millions of red, luminous eyeballs. If they were in a script, then this scene would be a cautious evacuation from a city about to be extinguished.

The radio's tale of a contemporary preparing to blast off into the afterlife sparks my imagination. I visualize the hand of an associate, trembling in his other land, the region between the Tigris and Euphrates rivers—and birthplace of writing—as it reaches under his vest, and connects two jerry-rigged wires.

My full gas tank could explode me into a heaven towards a fiery, setting sun that has come to mean paradise on postcards mailed from California—palm trees in silhouette.

In a flash, his body turns into a fine dust that filters the sunlight in his country. The discharge around his chest speeds him and the neighbors around his body home towards an eclipse of life. He believes that a full aliveness exists elsewhere, though unseen by the breathing. He, like so many religious zealots, sees the corporeal body as simply an earthen jar for the eternal spirit. Clay pots on store shelves shatter.

It is his way to retaliate against a seeming invasion of primordial, ceramic robots. They are Special Forces awaiting their instructions from America's commander-in-chief. Like Emperor Qin, I'm positive that our leader believes in the necessity of bringing an army with him into his afterlife too.

Perhaps both ancient and existing emperors consider shock-and-awe as the only viable doctrine to use, whether in life or death? The tremendous power and the stunning spectacles of not only 8,000 clay soldiers, but also now most probably clay missiles, will render helpless any other god's holy insurgents. Will American civilians still "support the troops," even if they battle in the afterlife with angels and the New Testament's God?

Peace is a false state of affairs, even in paradise. Diplomacy takes too long, even with eternity. □

Acknowledgments & Illustrations

Special Thanks to all of the artists involved and to *Arid Journal* Editors Greg Esser, Andrea Polli, and Kim Stringfellow; Arizona State University *Desert Initiative* Director Greg Esser; Armory Center of the Arts Gallery Director and Chief Curator Irene Tsatsos; *Artillery* magazine Editor Tulsa Kinney and Associate Editor Carrie Paterson; Blue West Books publishers Deborah Paes de Barros, Carlton Smith, and Mark Smith, and designer Ben Hatheway; Dick Hebdige, University of California, Santa Barbara; Fairleigh Brooks; KCET Director of Program Development and Production Juan Devis and KCET *Artbound* Managing Editor and Producer Drew Tewksbury; Eva Kirsch, Director, Robert and Frances Fullerton Museum of Art at CSUSB; Laguna Art Museum Director Bolton Colburn (1998-2011); Naida Osline; Palm Springs Art Museum Donna and Cargill MacMillan Jr. Director of Art Daniell Cornell and The Getty Foundation's initiative *Pacific Standard Time*; Roberts & Tilton Gallery Co-Owners Bennett and Julie Roberts; Scott Smith Miller; University of California Institute for Research in the Arts (UCIRA); UCR ARTSblock Executive Director Jonathan Green and UCR College of Humanities, Arts, and Social Sciences (CHASS) Dean Stephen Cullenberg, University of California, Riverside.

Essays published in similar versions appeared in:

Arid: A Journal of Desert Art, Design and Ecology: *Aridtopia's Loop Writing: A Desert Language; Repurposing the Los Angeles Aqueduct as a Pathway for Sacred Pilgrimages;* and *Secession in the Desert: How Walking through a Mock Iraqi City Led to Aridtopia.* **Arizona State University Art Museum**, Tempe, AZ: *Miguel Palma: An Artistic Exploration of the Sonoran Desert by a Human Alien,* exhibition catalog for *Miguel Palma: Trajectory*. **Armory Center of the Arts**, Pasadena, CA: *Manifest Destination in Spaceport America by Connie Samaras,* exhibition catalog for *Connie Samaras: Tales of Tomorrow.* **Artillery Magazine**, Los Angeles, CA: *Concrete Islands Along California Freeways Jump-Start a New Society; Presence Machines: Philip K. Dick's Roman Empire and The Imaginary 20th Century;* and *Visiting with China's Ancient Terra Cotta Warriors, or Combat-Ready for Paradise.* **KCET Artbound**, Los Angeles, CA: *A Reconsideration of Fourth of July Fireworks and Independence Day in Light of Cai Guo-Qiang's Sky Ladder; An Inland Empire Afterlife: The Immortality Project, Cryonics, and a 26-Foot Tall Marilyn Monroe; An Iron Worm Whistles In My Mind; Area 51: A Sound Installation by Venzha Christ; Considering the Sound of an Air Conditioner while Perusing John Cage: Zen Ox-Herding Pictures; Hell's Union: Motorcycle Club Cuts as American Folk Art; The Idyll-Beast: A Wild Child Imaginary in Idyllwild, California; Levitating the Archaic Mind with Michael Heizer's Levitated Mass;* and *Resurrection Machines of Ancient Egypt in San Bernardino and of Ancient Cinema in Hollywood.* **Laguna Art Museum**, Laguna Beach, CA: *Laurie Brown: Recent Terrains,* exhibition brochure. **Palm Springs Art Museum**, Palm Springs, CA: *From Beefcake to Skatecake: Shifting Depictions of Masculinity and the Backyard Swimming Pool in Southern California,* exhibition catalog for *Backyard Oasis: The Swimming Pool in Southern California Photography.* **Roberts & Tilton Gallery**, Los Angeles, CA: *Pump Up the Realism: Todd Brainard's Paintings,* exhibition catalog. **UCR ARTSblock**, Riverside, CA: *Cabins in the Desert: Ruminating on Kim Stringfellow's Exploration of Jackrabbit Homesteads,* exhibition brochure for *Jackrabbit Homestead: Tracing the Small Tract Act in the Southern California Landscape, 1938-2008, a project by Kim Stringfellow; Free Enterprise: The Art of Citizen Space Exploration,* exhibition catalog; and *Lewis deSoto & Erin Neff: Tahquitz,* exhibition brochure.

Illustrations   *(listed in order of appearance in the book)*

Title page: photograph by Tyler Stallings, view from inside the author's "MiniCooperMarsRover" looking forwards and backwards simultaneously at the Mojave Desert.

Secession in the Desert: How Walking through a Mock Iraqi City Led to Aridtopia: photographs by Tyler Stallings of Mock Iraqi city at Marine Corps Air Ground Combat Center in Twentynine Palms.

Aridtopia's Loop Writing: A Desert Language: photographs by Tyler Stallings, top: Ocotillo at night, bottom: kneeling woman, both images taken in Joshua Tree National Park.

Concrete Islands Along California Freeways Jump-Start a New Society: photographs by Naida Osline, top: concrete island as the 60, 91, 215 freeway interchange, Riverside, CA, bottom: concrete island at Avenue L exit off the 14 freeway, Landcaster, CA.

Repurposing the Los Angeles Aqueduct as a Pathway for Sacred Pilgrimages: handdrawn map by Tyler Stallings; photographs by Tyler Stallings from journey through Owens Valley, CA.

An Iron Worm Whistles In My Mind: photographs by Tyler Stallings of cargo train traversing the dry bed of the Santa Ana River, Riverside, CA, and old Union Pacific train engine on display in Freemont Park, Riverside, CA.

Considering the Sound of an Air Conditioner while Perusing *John Cage: Zen Ox-Herding Pictures*: top: *I Ching* hexagram, courtesy of Wikipedia Commons, bottom: photograph by Tyler Stallings of the air conditioning unit in the author's home.

Area 51: A Sound Installation by Venzha Christ: top: photograph by Anas Etan of Venzha Christ taking sound recordings around Area 51, bottom: photograph by Nikolay Maslov showing detail from *Area 51* installation at UCR ARTSblock.

Pump Up the Realism: Todd Brainard's Paintings: top: Todd Brainard, *Field 31*, 2002, oil on birch panel, 40 x 60 inches, courtesy of the artist, bottom: Todd Brainard, *Lot 57A: Southeast View*, 2002, oil on birch panel, 32 x 48 inches, courtesy of the artist.

Laurie Brown: Recent Terrains: top: Laurie Brown, *Recent Terrains #1, Laguna Hills, CA*, 1991, silver print, 34" x 49" courtesy of the artist, bottom: Laurie Brown, *Divining Western Waters #13*, 1995, Iris digital print, 24" x 30" courtesy of the artist.

Cabins in the Desert: Ruminating on Kim Stringfellow's Exploration of Jackrabbit Homesteads: top: Kim Stringfellow, *Brewer Homestead, U.S. Patent No. 1146096*, 2006-2008, photograph, courtesy of the artist, bottom: Kim Stringfellow, *Interior of Conzelman Homestead, U.S. Patent No. 1170083*, photograph courtesy of the artist.

From Beefcake to Skatecake: Shifting Depictions of Masculinity and the Backyard Swimming Pool in Southern California: photograph by Tyler Stallings of empty backyard swimming pool, Riverside, CA.

Free Enterprise: The Art of Citizen Space Exploration: top: Bradley Pitts, still image from the video installation *Singular Oscillations*, 2008. Pitts is floating and falling freely within the cabin of the Russian parabolic-flight aircraft with is eyes closed and ears blocked. The project is an exploration of trajectory and the empty volume of the plane in and of itself. Copyright 2008, Bradley Pitts Studio. All rights reserved, bottom image: photograph by Tyler Stallings of entrance to Mojave Air and Space Port, Mojave, CA.

Manifest Destination in Spaceport America by Connie Samaras: top: Connie Samaras, *Spaceport America: Terminal Entry*, 2010, archival inkjet print from film, 30x40, edition of 5, photo courtesy of the artist, bottom: Connie Samaras, *Spaceport America: Terminal Hanger Facility, Facing Mission Control*, 2010, archival inkjet print from film, 30x40, edition of 5, photo courtesy of the artist.

Miguel Palma: An Artistic Exploration of the Sonoran Desert by a Human Alien: top: Miguel Palma, *Trajectory* exhibition, *In Image We Trust*. 2011-2012, mixed media, kinetic installation, photo courtesy Arizona State University Art Museum. The sculpture featured a model of an F16 fighter jet jutting above the conglomeration of toys and domestic items with a small surveillance camera in its nose, bottom: Miguel Palma, *Trajectory* exhibition, repurposed 1985 M1008 CUCV troop carrier for exploring the Sonoran Desert as if on another planet, 2011-2012, photo courtesy of Arizona State University Art Museum.

A Reconsideration of Fourth of July Fireworks and Independence Day in Light of Cai Guo-Qiang's *Sky Ladder*: photographs by Tyler Stallings of Fourth of July fireworks shot from atop Mt. Rubidoux, Riverside, CA.

Presence Machines: Philip K. Dick's Roman Empire and The Imaginary 20th Century: top: photograph of ancient Roman Forum courtesy of Wikipedia Commons, bottom: photograph by Tyler Stallings of interior atrium of Bradbury Building, downtown Los Angeles, featured in the film *Bladerunner* that was based on Dick's novel, *Do Androids Dream of Electtric Sleep?*.

Levitating the Archaic Mind with Michael Heizer's *Levitated Mass*: photographs by Tyler Stallings, top: rock quarry in Riverside, CA where Heizer's rock was situated, and of La Brea Tar Pits, located near Los Angeles County Museum of Art.

The Idyll-Beast: A Wild Child Imaginary in Idyllwild, California: photographs by Tyler Stallings and courtesy of David Jerome of Idyll-Beast Museum, Idyllwild, CA.

Lewis deSoto & Erin Neff: *Tahquitz*: photograph by Lewis deSoto of installation at UCR ARTSblock: Lewis deSoto & Erin Neff, *Tahquitz*, 2012, sound, voice, foam, steel and fiberglass boulder, speakers, transparent map, glass gobo of Cahuilla basket design, Edison Home Phonograph (wax cylinder recorder/player), table for phonograph, tables for books, and video monitors. Photos courtesy of Lewis deSoto. Installation views at Culver Center of the Arts, University of California, Riverside.

Resurrection Machines of Ancient Egypt in San Bernardino and of Ancient Cinema in Hollywood: top: photograph of set design for *The Ten Commandments* built on the Guadalupe-Nipomo Dunes on the California coast in 1923, bottom: photograph of set of four canopic jars for Ankh-Payee-Heri, limestone, Egypt, 1085-715 B.C. RAFFMA, the Robert and Frances Fullerton Museum of Art at CSUSB. Permanent Egyptian Collection. Photo by Robert A. Whitehead/CSUSB.

An Inland Empire Afterlife: The Immortality Project, Cryonics, and a 26-Foot Tall Marilyn Monroe: photograph by Tyler Stallings of twenty-six foot tall Marilyn Monroe statue in Palm Springs, CA, *Forever Marilyn* by Seward Johnson.

Hell's Union: Motorcycle Club Cuts as American Folk Art: photograph by Jeff Decker of Hell's Union motorcycle club cut.

Visiting with China's Ancient Terra Cotta Warriors, or Combat-Ready for Paradise: top: photograph of Terra Cotta Warriors on display in China courtesy of Wikipedia Commons, bottom: photograph by Tyler Stallings of broken Terra Cotta Warrior on display at Bowers Museum, Santa Ana, CA. □

Index

A

Action Man, 158
Adam and Eve, 63
aerospace industry, 137, 161
Aetherius Society, 179
Afghan, *8*
Afghanistan, 154
Africa, 20, 49, 170
afterlife, 211
Agnes Meyer-Brandis, 143
Alabama Hills, 48
Alan Bacock, 43
Albert Bierstadt, 90
Alcor, 212
Alvino Siva, 195
American Cinematheque, 206
American dream, 131
American Motorcycle
    Association, 225
Amish quilts, 223
Anaheim, 162, 215
Ancient Bristlecone Pine, 46
Andrea Zittel, 105
Ansel Adams, 96
Anza Borrego, 193
apocalyptic, 91, 104, 163
Apollo 12, 142
Apollo program, 137
Arabian, *8*, 19, 31, 149
Area 51, 81
Aridtopia, 11, 17, 31
Arizona, 11, 17, 154, 158, 180,
    215
Arizona Highways, 155
Arizona State University Art
    Museum, 153
Arnold Schoenberg, 68

Art & Technology, 137
Art in the Streets, 117
Arthur Woods, 142
Asian, 19
Atacama, 31
Athletic Model Guild, 111
Atlanta, 127
Australia, 44
Australian, 20
avant-garde music, 63, 68
Aztec, 98

B

bachelor pad, 119
beefcake, 112
Benjamin Franklin, 136
Bernd and Hilda Becher, 97
Bible, 116, 187
Big Bang, 63
Big Pine, 42
Big Pine Paiute Tribe, 43
Bigfoot, 185
Bigfoot Field Researchers, 188
Bill Osgerby, 118
Bindibu, 20
Bishop, 42
Black Mountain College, 68
Blair Witch Project, 189
Bob Gentry, 112
Bob Mizer, 110, 111, 121
bodybuilding, 112
Bonanza, 102
Book of the Dead, 208
Boston, 127
Bowers Museum, 237
Boxcar Willie, 62
Bradley Pitts, 143
Brian Aldiss, 182

Brine-fly larvae, 39
British Empire, 161
Buckminster Fuller, 105
Bureau of Land Management, 103
Burlington Northern, 57

C

C'hing-chu, 73
Cacti, 14
Cahuilla, 36, 181, 193
Cahuilla Bird Singers, 194
Cai Guo-Qiang, 162
CalArts, 216
California, 31, 215, 238
California Leonardo da Vinci Discovery, 144
California Museum of Photography, 181, 197
California State University San Bernardino, 201, 219
California State University, Hayward, 41
cargo containers, 58
Carl Andre, 183
Carrie Paterson, 143
Case Study House, 109
Cecil B. DeMille, 207, 218
cement oases, 116
Center for Land Use Interpretation, 143
Cerro Gordo, 40
Chaco Canyon, 13
Charles Darwin, 136
Chicago, 8, 62, 217
Chihuahuan Desert, 21
China, 37, 73, 161, 237
China Lake, 37
Cholla, 14

Chris Burden, 180
Christian Waldvogel, 143
Christianity, 202, 211
cinéma vérité, 121
citizen scientist, 158
citrus, 58
civilian space travel, 135
clean water, 15
CNES, 142
Cold War, 149
Communism, 163
Connie Samaras, 143, 147
consumerism, 15, 109, 118
Corbusier, 168
cosmos, 50, 136
Craig Stecyk, 110, 115
Crater North, 154
cry dance, 47
cryonic hibernation, 212
Cultural Center of European Space Technologies, 144
Culver Center of the Arts, 81, 182, 193
Culver City, 114
Curators of Riverside, 234

D

D.T. Suzuki, 70
Dada, 82, 232
David "Honeyboy" Edwards, 62
David Hockney, 109
David Jerome, 185
David Tudor, 68
Dead Sea, 41
Death Valley, 39
Declaration of Independence, 161
Dennis Bell, 111

Department of Water and Power, 31
Desert Initiative: Desert One, 153
Desert Magazine, 103
deserthood, 38
Diane Agrest, 129
Dick Hebdige, 7
Disney, 162, 215
DogTown Z-Boy skateboard team, 110
Dragan Živadinov, 142
dreamdesert, 38
Dust Mitigation, 40
dystopian, 117, 182

E

Earthworks, 180
East Asian, 67
Easy Rider, 225
EchoStar XVI, 143
Ecoshack, 105
ecosystem, 11, 17, 188
Ecotopia, 10
Ed "Big Daddy" Roth, 225
Eden, 61, 103
Edenic California dream, 116
Edwards Air Force Base, 37, 138, 143
Eero Saarinen, 147
Egypt, 202
Egyptian, 8, 18, 177, 201, 219
Egyptian Theater, 205
Egyptomania, 205
El Segundo, 138
Endangered and Imaginary Creature Act, 186
Enlightenment, 187
Erin Neff, 193

eteam, 143
European Space Agency, 139
European Space Agency Topical Team Arts and Science, 144
extraterrestrial, 32, 58, 81, 137, 156

F

F. Valentine Hooven III, 114
family values, 109
FasTrak, 238
Fatty Arbuckle, 48
Felix Baumgartner, 155
Feral Park, 190
field recordings, 82
Final Frontier Design, 143
Fontana, 232
foreclosures, 131
Forever Marilyn, 217
Forrest Myers, 141
Fort Independence, 45
Fort Tejon, 46
Foster+Partners, 147
Fourth of July, 161
François Truffaut, 187
Frank Pietronigro, 143
Free Enterprise: The Art of Citizen Space Exploration, 135
Fresno, 131, 168
Frozen Walt Doll, 216
fulgurites, 41
Fullerton Museum, 201, 219
Future wars, 8
Futurism, 82, 233

G

Genesis, 187
genocide, 47

genome, 137
George Van Tassel, 83
Getting Loose, 118
GI Joe, 158
global capitalism, 147, 149
Gobi Desert, 48
gonzo journalism, 121
Grand Refusal of the Aqueduct, 43
Grand Secession, 12
Grauman's Chinese Theater, 205
gravity, 34, 143, 153, 161, 175, 194
Great Dry Cry, 48
Great Wall of China, 238
Greco-Roman, 204
Guadalupe Nipomo Dunes, 208
Gunga Din, 49
gunpowder, 161
Guy Rose, 90

H

Happening, 68
Harry and the Hendersons, 188
hedonism, 110
Hell's Angel, 224
Hell's Union: Motorcycle Club Cuts as American Folk Art, 223
hieroglyphics, 201
High Desert Test Sites, 105
Highway 215-North, 201
Highway 243, 186
Highway 62, 101
Hollywood, 109, 179, 205, 216, 219
Hollywood Boulevard, 205
Hollywood Forever Cemetery, 207
Holy Mountains, 179

home ownership, 131
homoerotic, 123
Hopalong Cassidy, 48
Horus, 204
House Beautiful, 111
Howard Carter, 205
Huckleberry Finn, 35
Hunter S. Thompson, 121

I

Iain Borden, 126
I-Ching, 70
ichthys, 169
Idyll-Beast, 185
Idyll-Beast Research Center Museum and Gift Shoppe, 186
Idyllwild, 185
Immortality Project, 212
Imperial Human, 15
Independence Day, 163
India, 48
Indian philosophy, 67
Indian Wells Valley, 37
indigenous, 149, 158
Indonesia, 81
Industrial Revolution, 59, 64
industrialization, 91, 232
Inland Empire, 131, 164, 185, 217
insecure man, 120
Integratron, 83
International Space Station, 135
Inyo White Mountains, 35
Iraq, *7, 154*
Isaac Newton, 136
Islam, 211

J

Jackrabbit Homestead, 101
James Cameron, 218
James Rosenquist, 92
Japanese rock garden, 71
Jawbone Canyon, 36
Jeff Decker, 223
Jeff Ho, 115
JFK Airport, 147
Johannes Kepler, 136
John Cage, 67
John Lomax, 82
John Martin Fischer, 211
John Sonsini, 124
John Templeton Foundation, 211
John Wayne, 48, 102
Johnny Cash, 62
Jonathan Rutherford, 119
Joshua Area, 83
Joshua Tree National Park, 18, 101
Julius Shulman, 109
Jurassic Park, 190
Jurupa Valley, 177
Juxtapoz art magazine, 116

K

Kaufmann House, 110
Keeler, 39
Kim Stringfellow, 101
King Tut, 203
Kitsou Dubois, 142
Kustum Kulture, 225

L

La Brea Tar Pits, 175

Laguna Beach High School, 232
Land art, 180
Land of many uses, 37
Las Vegas, 58, 205
Laurie Brown, 95
Leonardo da Vinci, 129
Levitated Mass, 175
Lewis Baltz, 97
Lewis deSoto, 181, 193
Lockheed Martin, 8
London, 118, 139, 176
Lone Pine, 42
Lone Pine Indian Reservation, 48
Lone Pine Museum of Film History, 48
Lone Ranger, 48
Long Beach, 178
Los Angeles Aqueduct, 31
Los Angeles County Museum of Art, 137, 175, 203
Los Angles, 31
Louis L'Amour, 102
Louvre Museum, 205
Lowry Burgess, 142
luminist painters, 91
lunar exploration, 138
Luxor Hotel, 205

M

Mammoth Lakes, 42
Manifest Destiny, 150
Mapping the Desert/Deserting the Map: An Interdisciplinary Response, 7
Marco Brambilla, 218
Marilyn Monroe, 218
Marine Corps Air Ground Combat Center, *7, 245*

Marko Peljhan, 135
Mars, 21, 32, 136, 143, 153, 156, 163, 219
Martian desert, 22
Martians, 22, 156, 163
masculine, 110
masculinity, 118
Max Yavno, 113
Mayan, 98
mesquite, 20
Mexican desert, 21
Mexico, 21, 180
Michael Govan, 177
Michael Heizer, 96, 175, 183
microgravity, 139
Middle East, 154
Midwest, 58
Miguel Palma, 153
Mike Parker Pearson, 176
mindfulness, 18, 64, 68
MiniCooperMarsRover, 39
MIR space station, 142
missionary, 47
Mississippi, 62
mock city, 7
moisture, 32, 69, 75
Mojave Air and Space Port, 138
Mojave Desert, *7, 17, 31, 33, 58*
Mono Lake, 41
Moon, 136, 143, 153, 156, 163
Moon Museum, 141
Mormon Tea, 19, 35
Morongo Basin, 101
Mount Rubidoux, 161, 219
Mount Whitney, 48
Mountain Lake Workshop, 67
Movie Road, 49
Mt. Slover, 197
mummies, 201
Muscle Beach, 113

Museum of Contemporary Art, 72, 116, 162, 180, 193
musique concrete, 63, 82

N

Napoleon Bonaparte, 205
NASA, 135, 156
NATO, 8
Naval Air Weapons Station China Lake, 39
Nazca Lines, 37
Nazi, 63, 227
Nejc Trošt, 144
Neolithic Age, 175
Nevada, 11, 17, 81, 84, 180
New Journalism, 121
New Mexico, 11, 17, 135, 143, 147, 180
New Orleans, 169
New School for Social Research, 70
New Topographics, 97
New York Times, 21
Nile, 19, 201
nineteenth century, 57, 95, 205
Noah Purifoy, 105
Northern California, 10
Numa, 36

O

Oakland, 232
oasis, 19, 131, 155
Ocotillo, 14
oil rig, 90
Olancha, 40
Olmec, 179
Orange County, 95, 162, 167, 215

Oregon, 10
orgy, 120
outlaw motorcycle clubs, 223
out-of-body experiences, 211
Owens River, 32
Owens Valley, 31
Owens Valley Paiute, 48
Owens Valley Paiute-Shoshone
    Cultural Center & Museum, 47
Ox-Herding Pictures, 67

P

Pacific Coast Highway, 207
Pacific Northwest, 187, 188
Pacific Standard Time, 130
Paiute, 32
Palm Desert, 7
Palm Springs, 103, 110, 193, 217
panoramic, 90, 92, 95
parabolic training flight, 143
paradise, 131, 239
Paramount Studios, 207
Passaic River, 182
Pearblossom, 33
Pennsylvania, 143
permaculture, 10
Persian Gulf, 170
pharaoh, 202
Philip K. Dick, 168
Phoenix, 127, 155
Photo League, 113
photorealist, 89
Physique Pictorial, 110
Pierre Henri Marie Schaeffer, 63,
    82
Playboy, 111, 119
Playboys in Paradise, 118
Pomona College Museum of Art,
    67

Portland Cement plant, 181
Portugal, 153
postwar era, 109
primal, 41, 120, 131, 183, 190
pyramids, 98, 202

Q

questionary, 47

R

Ra, 201, 204, 206
rattlesnake, 22, 37
Ray Kass, 70, 71
recycling, 10
Red Bull Stratos, 155
resurrection machines, 201
Richard Clar, 142
Richard Estes, 89
Riverside, 57, 98, 138, 161, 177,
    185, 197, 201, 212, 215, 232
Rob La Frenais, 142
Robert Adams, 97
Robert Bechtle, 89
Robert Ettinger, 212
Robert Heinlein, 156
Robert Smithson, 91, 96, 158,
    182
Roland Emmerich, 163
Rolywholyover A Circus, 72
Roman, 120, 129, 202
Roman Empire, 167, 169
Royal College of Art, 176

S

Sacramento, 48
sacred geography, 175
Saguaro, 14

Sahara, 19, 31
salt plains, 41
Salton Sea, 102
Salyut, 136
Sam Binkley, 118
San Bernardino, 103, 178, 181, 185, 197, 202, 232
San Jacinto Mountain, 194
San Luis Obispo, 207
San Pedro, 7, 58
Santa Fe Railroad, 57
Santa Monica Museum of Art, 218
Sasquatch, 185
Scarab, 204
science fiction, 104, 163, 182, 218
Scott Stine, 41
Scottsdale, 215
self-reliance, 130
SETI, 137
settler-DWP, 43
seventeenth century, 60
Seward Johnson, 217
Shangri-La, 131
shipping containers, 7, *12*
Sierra Nevada, 35
Silicon Valley, 138
siphon, 37
SkateBoarder magazine, 110
Skeith De Wine, 144
Skip Engblom, 115
Skylab, 136
Small Tract Act, 101
smallness, 106
Solar panels, 21
Sonny Barger, 232
Sonoran desert, 31, 153
South Africa, 44
South Coast Plaza, 168

southern California, 17, 32, 178
Southern California, 11, 101, 115, 138, 193
Southern California Institute of Architecture (SciArc), 105
southwest, 13
space exploration, 135
Space Shuttle, 136, 142
Space X, 135
Spaceport America, 143, 147
Spiral Jetty, 92, 96, 158
spiritual, 37, 60, 69, 97, 105, 136, 149, 154, 175, 179, 181, 198
spiritual geography, 69
Star City Gagarin Cosmonaut Training Center, 142
steady-state, 10
steam whistles, 59
stela, 206
Stephanie Smith, 105
stereographic, 98
Steve Reich, 63
Steve Roden, 82
Stonehenge, 175
Stonehenge Riverside Project, 176
Stonewall riot, 123
Stranger in a Strange Land, 156
sublime, 90
sub-orbital flight, 138
succulents, 14
Sun, 75, 201
Sun Agreement, 14
sun god, 18, 206
Sunset Boulevard, 207
surf shop, 121
sustainability, 10, 31
swimming pool, 110
Syria, 8, 205
Syrian Desert, 8

T

Tahquitz, 193
Tahquitz Canyon Way, 217
Taschen, 114
Tehachapi Pass Wind Farm, 36
Ten Commandments, 208
Terra Cotta Warriors, 237
The Arts Catalyst, 139
The Grove, 168
The Imaginary 20th Century, 167
Thirteen United States, 12
Thom Fitzgerald, 128
Thomas van Leeuwen, 110
time capsules, 104
Titan, 32, 136
Todd Brainard, 89
Tomorrowland, 216
train, 57
train whistle constant, 58
Train whistles, 59
Trans World Flight Center, 147
transcontinental rail lines, 57
Trevor Paglen, 143
Trieste Constructivist Cabinet, 141
Tuareg, 20
twenty-first century, 95
Twentynine Palms, *7*, *101*

U

U.S. Post Office, 125
U.S. Route 14, 36
U.S. Route 18, 33
U.S. Route 395, 39, 42, 48
U.S. Supreme Court, 112, 123
UCLA, 83
UCR ARTSblock, 81, 140, 223
UFO, 81, 148

underworld, 18, 201, 206
Union Pacific Railroad, 58
University of California, Riverside, 81, 211
University of California, Santa Barbara, 7
Urban Operations Training Systems, 8
Utah, 96, 180
utopia, 105
utopian, 10, 17, 31, 139, 148, 211

V

Valencia, 216
Valentine Michael Smith, 156
Venice beach, 113
Venus, 136
Venzha Christ, 81
Victor of Aveyron, 187
Victoria Gardens, 168
Victoria Vesna, 83
Virgin Galactic, 135, 156
Virginia Dwan Gallery, 183
Vitruvius, 129

W

Wales, 176
Wall Street, 227
Walter De Maria, 183
Washington, 10
water, 10, 32
water baby, 49
water rights, 33
Watts Tower Art Center, 105
Wayne Stanley, 113
Western Project Gallery, 114
Whole Earth Catalog, 122

Wild West, 105
Wonder Valley, 101

X

XCOR Aerospace, 135, 141, 143, 156

Z

Zen Buddhism, 67
Zephyr Productions, 115
Zombie, 216
Zooniverse, 137

About the Author

Tyler Stallings is the editor and contributor to numerous books on art and culture that focus on identity, technology, photography, popular culture, and desert studies. His books include *Free Enterprise: The Art of Citizen Space Exploration, Absurd Recreation: Contemporary Art from China, Truthiness: Photography as Sculpture, The Signs Pile Up: Paintings by Pedro Álvarez, Whiteness, A Wayward Construction, Desmothernismo: Ruben Ortiz Torres,* and *Uncontrollable Bodies: Testimonies of Identity and Culture.* He has been a contributing author to many other books including *The Great Picture: The World's Largest Photograph & the Legacy Project, Backyard Oasis: The Swimming Pool in Southern California Photography, 1945-1980, Surf Culture: The Art History of Surfing,* and *Mexico at the Hour of Combat: Sabino Osuna's Photographs of the Mexican Revolution.* He is a columnist for KCET-TV's *Artbound* program, and is the Artistic Director at Culver Center of the Arts and Director of Sweeney Art Gallery at University of California, Riverside.

See author website for Study and Book Club Guide.

www.tylerstallings.com

CPSIA information can be obtained at www.ICGtesting.com
Printed in the USA
BVOW11s0206280314

349052BV00003B/3/P